Cheers!
AW 2015

# OREGON WINE

# PIONEERS

**Vine Lives Publishing**
Portland, Oregon

Cover photo: Vineyards at Ghost Hill Cellars by Cila Warncke.

A to Z, Björnson, Coelho, Ghost Hill, Left Coast, Montinore, Ponzi, Whistling Dog photos by Cila Warncke.

Additional photos provided by Abacela, Adelsheim, A Blooming Hill, Dominio IV, Elk Cove, Illahe.

Additional photos for Adelsheim, A Blooming Hill, and Illahe by Tesan Warncke.

Original illustrations by Tesan Warncke.

Concept, design, and editing by Tesan & Ersun Warncke.

Photo editing by Carolina & Ersun Warncke.

Published by Vine Lives Publishing. Portland, Oregon.

Copyright © 2015 by Cila Warncke. All rights reserved.

Printed in the United States.

ISBN 978-1-943090-76-1

*For Carl*

———————

*To Paul H
all warmest*

# Contents

**Wineries & Vineyards**

Björnson .............................................................................. 10
Adelsheim ........................................................................... 22
Elk Cove .............................................................................. 34
A to Z Wineworks ............................................................... 46
Ponzi .................................................................................... 60
Montinore ........................................................................... 72
Ghost Hill Cellars ............................................................... 84
Whistling Dog Cellars ....................................................... 98
Abacela ............................................................................... 110
A Blooming Hill ................................................................. 122
Illahe ................................................................................... 136
Coelho ................................................................................. 148
Left Coast Cellars .............................................................. 162
Dominio IV ......................................................................... 176
Plum Hill ............................................................................. 188

**Trail Guides**

Portland .............................................................................. 204
Forest Grove ....................................................................... 206
Newburg .............................................................................. 212
McMinnville ........................................................................ 218
Salem ................................................................................... 222
Southern Oregon ............................................................... 228

*O*regon Wine Pioneers aims to tell a good story and inspire you to take part in that story. We hope you take it along when you head out to visit the wineries and vineyards featured on its pages.

With that in mind, we have included Trail Guides with maps and directions to help you on your way. Fine wine is best appreciated with great food so we asked the winemakers to recommend the best restaurants in their respective areas.

You will find a blank page alongside the tasting notes for each winery. Fill it in with your own tasting notes and get an autograph while you are there! (If you visit all 15 be sure to let us know.)

Join our private, ad-free online community @ https://vineliv.es. We would love to hear about your experiences in wine country. At Vineliv.es you can share your stories and photos, ask questions, get news and event updates, and enjoy exclusive content.

Oregon Wine Pioneers showcases a fraction of the state's 400-plus vineyards and wineries, each with a unique story and ethos. We hope this book serves as an introduction that will inspire you to explore and discover more of the exciting world of Oregon wine.

*Bon Voyage*

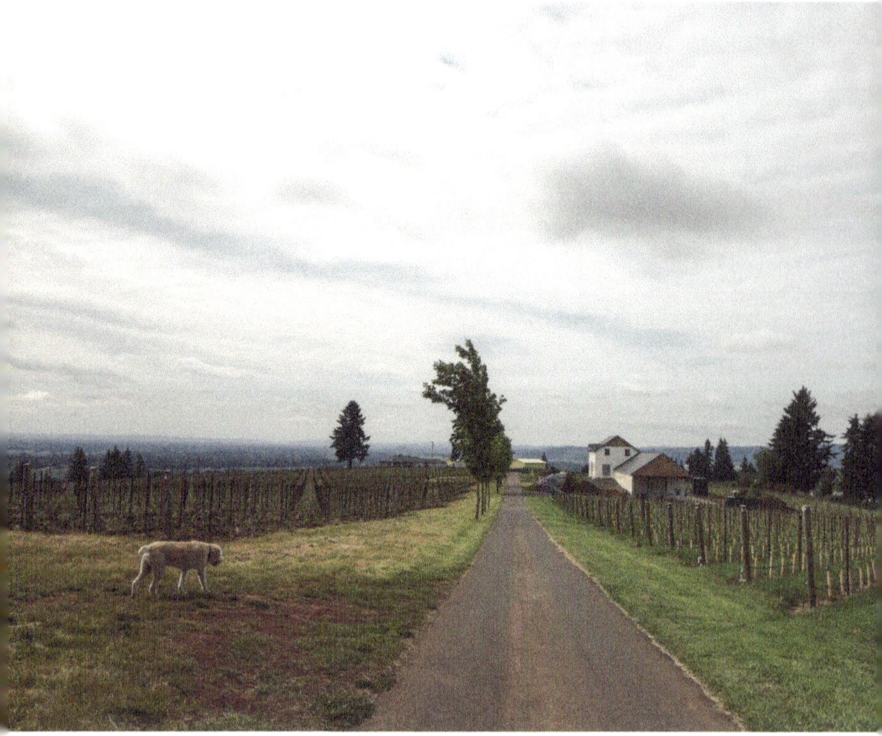

# Björnson

Memorial Day weekend is the quasi-official beginning of Willamette Valley wine season. Wineries large and small spring-clean and unpack cases of their best vintages in preparation for an influx of holiday visitors. Saturday will be a busy day at Björnson Vineyard. Winemaker Pattie Björnson and an assistant arrange bottles on a table covered with charcoal cloth. Twin Stars and Stripes flutter above a red-topped table where Pattie sets the cash box. A caterer arrives with a basket from Willamette Valley Cheese Company in nearby Salem. Sliced meats, crackers, and olives are laid out. Pattie and Mark's teenage son Hunter slides out the front door and, ignoring the bustle, hops on his bike and takes off. The land falls swift and fast from the 530-foot elevation of the house, through the vineyards, past the shell of the winery and tasting room, still under construction.

It is early. No sound but birds trilling in the cool, still air. Mark Björnson and Thor, their hundred-pound white labradoodle, walk me through the vineyards. Slender fingers of vine curl around taut trellis wires, fluttering green across the criss-cross pattern of silver. "How many feet of wire per acre?" Mark calculates: "In an acre you have 5500 feet, times eight wires. That's 44,000 feet, so eight or nine miles on every acre. On 28 acres we have, uh, 250 miles of wire, on this site. I'd never thought of that before."

Not many details get past Mark. He weaves together family anecdotes, explanations of grape DNA and a quick geology lesson as we approach the half-finished winery. Soon Björnson's production will move under this soaring roof. He throws open a door to light the cavernous production area, pointing out the insulating properties of the waffle-grid concrete walls and the layout with the barrel room dug into the side of the hill. "The concrete footings are underground to transmit the ground temperature through the walls. That will regulate the building to about 57 degrees," Mark says. "It will hold its temperature beautifully – no need for heating or cooling." He walks me through the lab where they'll test wine for sulphite and alcohol levels, and points out the "enormously expensive" automated sprinkler system. "Wine doesn't burn very well, but oh well."

A joke, obviously, but delivered with such dry nonchalance it almost slips past. His deadpan tone reminds me of the wry jokes I heard on a visit to Reykjavik. Even as a second-generation American, Mark has an Icelandic sense of humor.

Mark's great-grandparents immigrated from Iceland to Canada, where his grandparents were born. When his grandfather was a seven-year-old he walked with his father from north of Winnipeg several hundred miles south to North Dakota to claim a homestead. Eventually the whole family came to the US. Mark's father was born in North Dakota in 1910, though he spoke only Icelandic till he went to school.

Farming is Pattie's heritage too, making their move from white-collar careers in Minneapolis to Oregon agriculture less surprising. Her family, the Knights, immigrated from Kent, England to Minnesota in 1857. As a child, Pattie moved from Minneapolis to a farm community called Owatonna, MN. "I grew up in the Valley of the Jolly Green Giant," she jokes. "When I was 18 I wanted nothing to do with farming. Now, on our vineyard, I can't imagine living anywhere else. I love the cycle of farming."

Love for the land and pioneer grit helped Mark and Pattie get through the long days involved in turning a stony shoulder of the Eola-Amity Hills into a fruitful vineyard. Before they could plant the vines they had to pull more than 1000 tons of rock out of the earth. "We took about 300 tons off just this hill," Mark says, describing weeks shifting boulders with an excavator, using a tractor to remove smaller ones, and tilling with a field-cultivator to clear pebbles till they hauled away 35 dump truck loads. Finally, they drilled stakes into the chunks that were too big to move, turning them into part of the infrastructure of the vineyard.

The vineyards are young, but growing fast. "Each one is like a child," Pattie says. The youngsters love the rugged basalt soil, laid down by the volcanic eruptions that created the Columbia River basalt group some 15 million years ago. The Björnson's first planting was in 2006; their vines grow rapidly and fruit profusely. Twenty-eight acres are planted now: mostly Pinot, plus Chardonnay, Auxerrois, and Gamay Noir.

Mark explains the genetic relationship of sister grapes Chardonnay and Auxerrois, the 2500 year history of Pinot, and the story of the lesser-known Gamay: "In the 1400s the Duke of Burgundy made it a capital offence to grow Gamay Noir. The peasants loved it and he was trying to stop them growing. Being a good peasant,

I plant some Gamay." For Mark, like the Burgundian peasants, it is a valuable crop. It yields up to nine tons an acre versus Pinot Noir's two-and-a-half, and Mark sells it to other local wineries. "It's lighter than Pinot and very enjoyable. You can use it to make a good, $15 summer red."

Pattie and Mark, like all self-funded winemakers, have to balance finance, farm and family. Mark still works full time in the health insurance field ("You know those evil MBAs who make insurance decisions? I'm one of those"). Pattie was a computer programmer before studying winemaking at Chemeketa, and puts her skills to work managing the technical, administrative and marketing aspects of the vineyard. Their four children: Kaitlyn, Kristjan, Claire and Hunter, are enmeshed in the winery.

Kaitlyn was a toddler when she accompanied Mark and Pattie on a tandem bike across Europe in the early 90s. They stopped along the way so Mark could volunteer during grape harvest in Germany's Mosel River valley. "I'd always wanted to have a farm," says Mark. "After that, I wanted a vineyard." By the time they moved to Oregon, Kaitlyn was a teenager and disinclined to pitch in moving rocks. Her 12-year-old brother Kristjan's enthusiasm won him the honor of having the first block of vines named after him. In time, Kaitlyn, Claire and Hunter got their own blocks. Kaitlyn, a chemical engineering student at Oregon State University, now lends Mark a hand with engineering work like wiring the barn for lights, plumbing and irrigation. "She's off to do an internship at a big cheese factory in California," her dad beams. "Really, winemaking is chemical engineering, it's the same kind of thing."

He reckons Kaitlyn may be the child to take over from Pattie as winemaker, which could make Björnson a pioneering mother-daughter vintner team. Hunter, the youngest, loves the outdoors – he might step into a viticulture role one day.

"I hope the kids are proud," says Pattie. "I hope we set a good example."

"They just think we're crazy," her husband grins.

"I talked to French winemakers and they looked at me like I was crazy," Pattie muses, recalling a family trip in 2004. "In France it's virtually impossible to come from a background with no experience and start a winery. I'm grateful we live in the United States and have so many opportunities. We sometimes take that for granted but it's remarkable. I want the kids to see that you can do pretty much anything you want, if you work hard at it."

It is refreshing to hear this American mantra from someone who is living it, rather than a politician trying to score points. Nice to be reminded that there are places (overlooked and under-reported) where hard work and good-humored determination still shape the land.

The first guests pull into the black-top parking area. A young couple approaches the tasting table, hip and androgynous in almost-matching skinny jeans and chunky glasses. Pattie, who found a minute to swap her "football mom" tee-shirt for a crisp white button-down, greets them, asks where they're from, and recommends a wine merchant in their Seattle neighborhood.

Mark is pouring glasses of Isabel Barrel Selection Pinot Noir (named for his grandmother) for an older couple and their friend: "This comes from that little block right here by the house. You notice it's on an eastern slope. Most of the rest of our vineyards are on a western slope and it's produced some different characteristics in the wine."

The trio sips and chats, revealing thick accents.

"Ah, Zurich," Mark says. "No, but I've been to Lucerne and I biked up to Interlaken." The guests drink then discuss in German, eventually choosing a bottle of 2012 Pinot.

Pattie is a purist winemaker: "We're gentle and do very minimal additions. We want the wines to be as transparent as possible."

This ethos extends to their agricultural practices too. Björnson Vineyard is LIVE certified and they are dedicated to retaining much of the original forest for plant diversity and wildlife. Mark sums up their goals as: "Care for the land. Make exceptional wine. Enjoy the journey."

More visitors approach, bubbling with holiday

weekend cheer, eager for a taste of Oregon. They've come to the right place. Nothing is more evocative of Oregon's past and future than a family that came from Iceland via Canada, North Dakota and Minnesota to make wine that could only come from the Willamette Valley.

For the Salem Trail Guide turn to Page 222.

# Björnson Tasting Notes

**Björnson Vineyard Pinot Noir 2012**

Clear ruby red color. Medium body. Strong cherry fruit with blackberry, juicy, springy, with rounded tannins.

**Björnson Vineyard Isabel Barrel Selection 2012**

Deep color. Medium body. Dark fruit, plum and blackcurrant with petrol notes. Reveals cherry and vanilla as it breathes.

**Haden Fig Pinot Noir 2012**

Made by Haden Fig winery from Björnson grapes. Medium color. Rounded body. Bright cherry and red fruits with notes of earth and spice.

**Haden Fig Chardonnay 2012**

Made by Haden Fig winery from Björnson grapes. Medium body. Ripe apple and pear with a hint of mineral in the finish. Slightly spiky.

ADELSHEIM
VINEYARD
40th Anniversary
TASTING ROOM
OPEN – Please come in!
Hours: 11am – 4pm
Daily

# Adelsheim

A delsheim is one of the Willamette Valley's oldest wineries. David and Ginny Adelsheim recruited friends and neighbors to help them plant their first vines in 1972 – long before Oregon Pinot Noir was a twinkle in the eye of even the most far-sighted wine buff or critic. Forty-two years is a long time in the Oregon wine business but a mere moment in the wider world of viticulture. The paradox of the Willamette Valley wine industry is that no matter how old it gets, it remains a newcomer.

A bank of solar panels the color of an oil-slick reflects hot bolts of light back toward the midday sky. Behind them looms a vast stone-clad building with a many-windowed central tower and two sprawling wings. As I open my car door a shrill cry stops me. Peering down I see a small brown bird a few feet away, braced on tiny claws, barred tail spread like a fan. She repeats the cry. A low shrub borders the parking lot and, assuming her babies are tucked in the foliage, I beat a respectful retreat. Catherine Douglas, manager of export sales, meets me, smiling, and indicates David has just arrived, driving a Subaru with special Wine Country plates (a $30 DMV surcharge). Compact and energetic, David briskly leads the way to the winery. His beard is white and trimmed closer than it was 40 years ago but, apart from that, it's easy to picture him tramping the vineyards all day.

The tasting room is airy, high-ceilinged and oozes modern good taste, as does the conference room where we settle. It is a little lonely with just three of us at one end of the gleaming wooden table but the half-dozen balloon-shaped Pinot Noir glasses ranged in front of us make our corner festive.

My prepared questions, however, lay stale on the page. Asking about the '70s feels akin to having an audience with Bob Dylan and requesting 'Hey Mr Tambourine Man'. I can read facts on the website. What I want to know is: What next? Once you've arrived where do you go?

Fortunately, this is on David's mind too: "The big question is: what happened? Why did a certain generation think winemaking would be intellectually challenging enough to make it worthwhile for these well-educated people to spend their lives creating this industry?" He pauses and looks at me as if expecting an answer: "Is there an intellectual challenge that continues to attract bright, entrepreneurial leaders? Or is this a one or two generation deal that carries on but doesn't have the intellectual attraction?"

When David and his wife Ginny purchased their first acres in the north Willamette Valley, in the shadow of the Chehalem Mountains, in 1971 the "intellectual attraction" was a complete leap into the unknown, arrived at in desultory fashion. David graduated from college with a degree in German literature but didn't have a particular aim in life. He did a stint in the Army. After his discharge he and Ginny traveled across Russia, then spent a summer in Europe. They discovered cultures that celebrated the connection between food and the land: "The idea that food could have intellectual importance was ground-breaking to us." There was no clear way to incorporate this revelation into their lives, though. They moved back to Oregon and David took a series of jobs that "made no sense". What did make sense was land.

"It was that '60s and '70s generation," he says. "We had this idea that going back to the land was a very honest thing. That you, an individual, could control everything from planting the vines to selling the wine, and do everything yourself, every step of the way."

We often call this the hippie generation but David and Ginny, and the other founding families of Oregon's wine industry, don't fit the "turn on, tune in and drop out" stereotype. They are idealistic and iconoclastic. They are determined, hard-working and relentless autodidacts. They went back to the land as pioneers, not pastoral fantasists.

For the Adelsheims this meant a literal do-it-yourself ethic. "You had to learn to do the electricity and plumbing for your house, how to rewire a press from Germany so it would run in the States. All those things," David says, slipping modestly into the second-person. What he means is he had to learn those things – plus how to plant and tend a vineyard, how to make wine, how to supervise construction of a winery and, not least, how to sell this novel concoction, Oregon Wine, to a state and nation that was largely ignorant of viticulture.

The story of Willamette Valley wine is, in part, a story of the frontier coming of age. David's father was a government lawyer, his mother the first woman to head Oregon's Democratic party, but even their sophisticated social circle was ignorant of wine. "My father's idea of wine was a sparkling Burgundy we had at Christmas," says David. "Partly because of Prohibition, partly because we were amateurs, we were new to the world of fine things."

Oregon's neophyte wine-makers didn't just have to achieve a level of quality; they had to define it. David recalls "sitting around tables at someone's rented house, drinking cheap Californian wine, trying to envision what a quality wine industry would look like – without being able to use any of those words properly." The Adelsheims and a dozen other families, including the Campbells from Elk Cove, were a nucleus of visionaries building a future whose existence depended entirely on their own efforts. A few decades later it is easy to gloss over that early period (the Adelsheim web timeline skips merrily from its first planting in '72 to its first commercial vintage in '78) but those were uncertain years. Like pioneers crossing the plains, they must have wondered if they were ever going to reach a discernible destination.

But they pushed on, working together, learning from each other's triumphs and mistakes, and seizing any opportunity to create a space for the fruits of their labours. David worked as a sommelier at L'Omelette restaurant in Portland in the '70s and created the first wine list with an Oregon-only section. Locals were nonplussed, though out-of-state visitors were eager to try the wines. It wasn't until the mid-80s that Oregon wine started to gain wider attention, giving the Adelsheims and their contemporaries a glimpse of its potential. "It's mind-blowing, given how naïve we were, that we have an industry you can read about in the UK or China, in glowing terms," he says. "An industry that is admired, copied, praised."

David returns to his question: What is the

next intellectual challenge? What's as hard as building something from scratch, relying only on your wits and the Whole Earth catalogue? Maybe nothing. By definition, there can only be one group of pioneers. Everyone who comes after is traversing known territory. But that doesn't mean there isn't value in the journey. Having surmounted the obstacles of simple survival and spreading the word, the Adelsheims continue to find new ways to break ground.

The winery and vineyard are both LIVE certified, which makes sense given David's passion for precision. He plainly loves the fact that this sustainability protocol is "not uncomplicated" and covers everything from waste disposal to land-use to generating electricity (which explains the solar panels). It requires wineries to achieve "ever-increasing scores" against its wide-ranging standards, which is the kind of pressure he seems to enjoy. They've built other self-imposed challenges into the business. For example, Adelsheim does up to 180 fermentations per harvest, fermenting its Pinot in batches of two to eight tons – a rare, labor-intensive process for a winery making 40,000 cases per year. And there's David's role in the industry, including work on importing new clones, establishing regulations, helping found events like the International Pinot Noir Celebration and Oregon Pinot Camp, and many years of service on the Oregon Wine Board.

Catherine discreetly pours wine. We pause to swirl and sip. David says the next step is to transform Adelsheim into "something closer to a luxury brand… it's what Oregon demands if you're going to have a viable business. We haven't figured out all the steps that are required." Problem solving is the lifeblood of Adelsheim. Winemaking was a way for David and Ginny to explore a changing culture and harness their fiery intellects in service of something tangible, sustainable and beautiful. They'll take the success, respect, and glowing reviews, thanks very much, but the real thrill, the thing that drives them, is the satisfaction of doing something no one did before.

After our interview David gathers the used glasses and disappears into the kitchen. I chat to the tasting room assistant and admire Ginny's artwork on the wall. David reappears: "Here," he says, putting a single strawberry in my hand. "It's the first of the season."

Its fresh sweetness bursts in my mouth, chasing the rich cherry and blackberry notes of the Pinot Noir we just tasted. "Wow," is all I can say. He smiles, nods and vanishes.

Outside it's 90 degrees. The air is rich with the perfume of flowers and faint, fresh notes of green blowing down from the vineyards. The Chehalem Mountains are blue against the sky. The parking lot is empty except for the small brown bird. Her presence opposite the high-tech panels is fitting – a gentle reminder that, for all its polish, Adelsheim is still rooted in the land.

For the Newberg Trail Guide turn to Page 212.

# Adelsheim Tasting Notes

**Adelsheim Caitlin's Reserve Chardonnay 2012**
Medium body. Very fresh. Honeyed peach with hint of green fig and fresh lemon.

**Adelsheim Elizabeth's Reserve Pinot Noir 2011**
Medium-light body. Soft, round berry nose. Slightly spiky raspberry, redcurrant and bright fruit. Blooms in the mouth.

**Adelsheim Boulder Bluff Pinot Noir 2011**
Medium body. Spicy nose. Blackberry and soft dark fruit, hint of spice. Lively on the tongue

**Adelsheim Ribbon Springs Pinot Noir 2011**
Rounded nose. Spicy but not too pungent. Red fruit, blackcurrant, high tannin but light in the mouth.

**Adelsheim Calkins Lane Pinot Noir 2011**
Medium body. Smooth mouthfeel. Dark juicy fruit, earthy with a hint of burnt sugar.

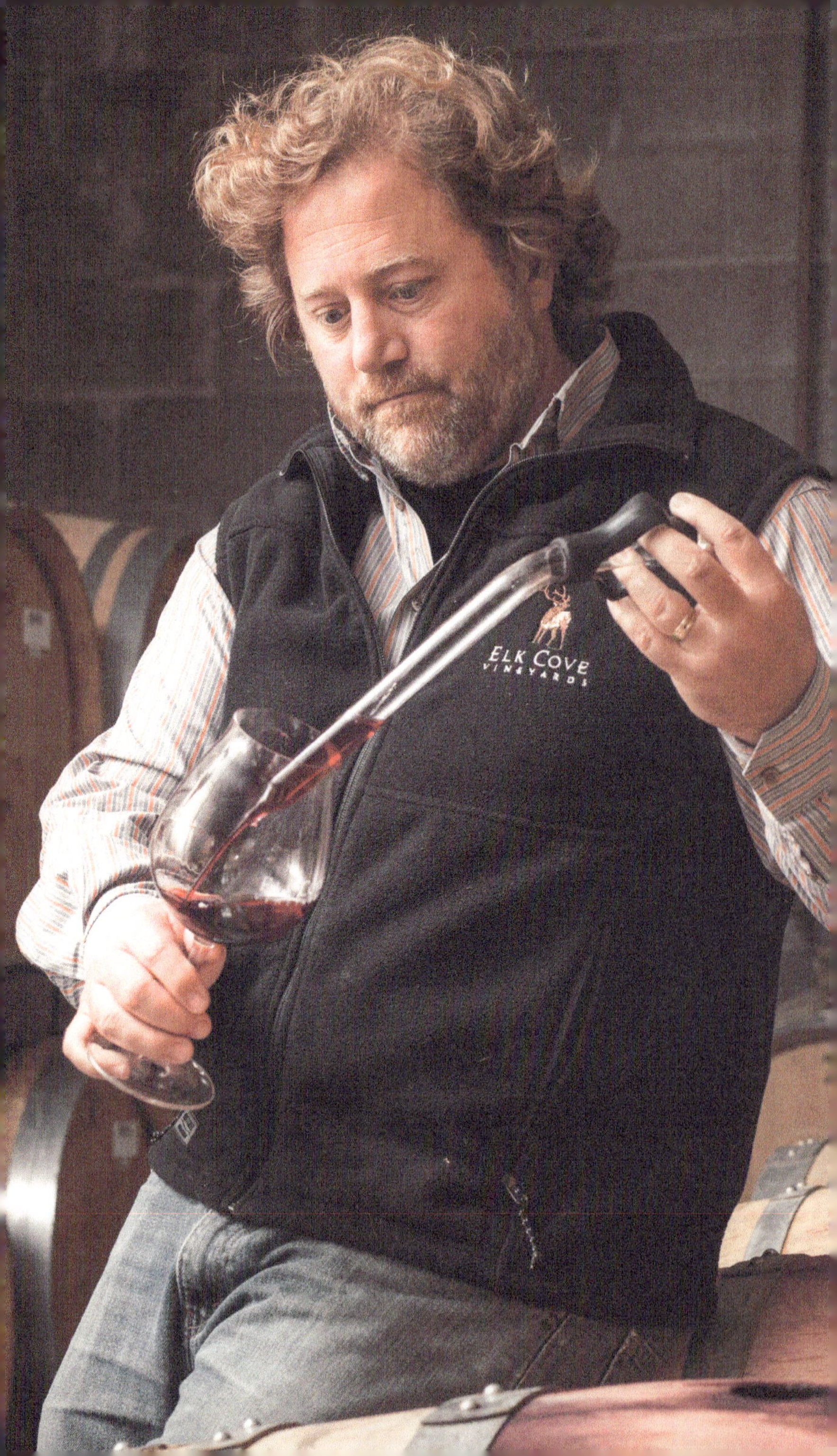

ELK COVE
VINEYARDS

# Elk Cove

Anna is Elk Cove founders Pat and Joe Campbell's youngest child. She meets me outside the bright, modern tasting room and, as we walk, points out the landmarks of her childhood domain. These days visitors flock to the Elk Cove estate near Gaston to appreciate the bucolic setting and extraordinary vintages that made it a *Wine & Spirits* Winery of the Year 2013. She remembers when it was an untamed slice of land, the perfect playground for a kid who loved the woods.

Anna shows me where their first house stood, the one her parents built from scrap lumber using a do-it-yourself book. Though basic, it was an improvement on the trailer they lived in when they arrived in 1974, drawn by Pat and Joe's theory that the steep, rocky hillsides that thwarted attempts to grow cherries, wheat and hazelnuts would be ideal for wine grapes.

Agriculture – as any farmer will tell you – is a gamble with long odds, short windows of opportunity and seemingly interminable waits for results. "It was probably 20 years before you could call the business successful," Anna muses. Twenty years of planting, pruning, trellising, picking, winemaking, bottling and marketing with no guarantee of the outcome.

Fortunately for wine-lovers, Pat and Joe Campbell are inclined to patience. They dated briefly in high school – Pat's parents farmed an orchard in Parkdale near Joe's home town of Hood River – but went separate ways. Joe attended Harvard and Stanford medical school, then married and had two children. It was only later that he and Pat encountered each other again, wed, and embarked on the "crazy dream" of creating one of Oregon's first wineries. Anna, siblings Eartha and Adam, and her half-brothers were an integral part of the project from the beginning. "Five kids is lots of labor," she quips. When she wasn't playing, disrupting quail hunts, or at school, she and the others pitched in picking grapes, bottling, and doing chores.

Anna and I catch up with Adam – winemaker since '95, big brother since forever – and find a quiet spot to talk in a banquet room. There is a strong family resemblance. Both have strawberry blond hair, though Adam's is peppered with grey. He has blue eyes; Anna's are almost the exact color of the olive-green stones in her earrings.

Adam's memories stretch back to the beginning of his family's homesteading adventure: "We had cows, horses, pigs, chickens. It was an 'all hands on deck' farmstead." Adam recalls their mom dashing out the door during lunch to greet potential customers, the constant demands of work, the long dinners at Nick's restaurant in McMinnville – the favorite haunt of Willamette Valley's wine pioneers: "As a kid I'd be sleeping under the table while dinners went on for hours, everyone tasting each other's wines, giving each other encouragement and ideas." It was a beautiful place to grow up, they agree; a busy, rich life, but not their life.

"When you're 18 you don't want to do what your parents did," says Adam. "My parents said, 'do whatever will keep you in school', so I have a degree in political science."

Anna studied biology then joined the Peace Corp and spent two years teaching science in Burkina Faso. Eventually she returned to Oregon and tried her hand at wine production for a while. "It wasn't a good fit." Ultimately, photography took her interest. She started working with a family friend, assisting on commercial shoots, then moved into wedding photos and portraiture.

"Our parents were good at not pressuring us to go into the business," Adam notes. Again, patience paid off. After university he returned to Elk Cove and started making wine with his father. Continuing in the "great history" of self-taught Oregon winemakers, he learned on the job, working side by side with Joe. Having grown up in the vineyards, Adam retains a deep respect for agriculture. "Having full control of the process, from grape to bottle, is the pinnacle of winemaking. I spend a lot of time in the vineyard, not just at harvest, but the whole season. Everything you see out there, if you are thoughtful, will inform your decisions about how you make the wines."

We sit overlooking a vineyard block straight out of a Van Gogh painting: lime-green stripes interspersed with thick strokes of scarlet. Anna has an aesthete's enthusiasm for the view – "Be sure to get some photos," she urges. Adam smiles. As much as he enjoys the image drawn by alternating rows of grapevines and red clover he is focused on the practical outcome: "What we're doing is growing our own nitrogen. It's beautiful but honestly, I can't wait to see the clover plowed in. That means it's going to start doing its job."

Using cover crops to enrich the soil is just one

of Elk Cove's many sustainable practices. The vineyard is certified Salmon Safe; they use solar power and biodiesel; a significant proportion of the 40,000 cases they produce each year is bottled in lighter-weight 'eco-glass'; white wine comes with environmentally friendly screw-tops; most importantly they provide healthcare and retirement funds for all their employees, including the vineyard workers. "Healthcare is a big issue," Adam notes. In addition to insuring their own employees, they are active supporters of ¡Salud! an organisation founded by doctors and winemakers to provide healthcare for seasonal workers – including a mobile clinic, dental care and help accessing additional medical services.

It is all part of what Adam calls, "A broader view of sustainability. Not just in terms of the vineyard, but in terms of the whole business, taking care of the folks here, and creating a valuable product we can ship around the states, and the world, and bring tax dollars back to Oregon."

Sustainability began at home for the Campbells. Everything they do is linked to the larger purpose of nurturing not just the business and profits, but a way of life. "Most of my family is in agriculture," Anna tells me later as we hike along the La Boheme block (her maternal great-grandparents made wine, pre-Prohibition). "A lot of farm families have really struggled over the past 50 years, trying to keep the land. It's great to see the wine industry making that possible." What she doesn't add, though she might, is that the industry has grown to support a diverse array of talent. She found her perfect role in the business as Elk Cove's creative director, bringing her photography skills and artist's eye to marketing and communications. While her brother tells the story of the land through wine, Anna renders it visually, giving visitors a different way to experience Oregon wine country. At the moment she is doing a time-lapse photo project capturing the vines as they bloom.

We continue down the hill into a block gridded with half-gallon waxed cardboard milk cartons (regular and chocolate). They're a biodegradable alternative to the plastic chutes commonly used to protect new plants. I squat to peer inside: the vines are tiny brown ropes, like packing twine, wrapped around the stakes. One or two precocious starts have run up a green flag of a leaf.

They hope this new planting will mimic – expand upon – the quality of Roosevelt, a 2.6 acre snippet of organically farmed, hand-maintained vineyard that produces "the best of the best" Pinot Noir. The winery's prize plot was named for the type of elk that still visit from time to time. With only 50 out of 200 acres planted there is plenty of wilderness here for deer, bear, bobcats, raptors, vultures, bald eagles, and countless smaller species of birds and mammals to thrive. The Campbells bought parcels of land around the Willamette Valley to create the Windhill, Clay Court, Mount Richmond and Five Mountain vineyards, allowing them to increase production but leave the original estate semi-wild.

"Because of the grapes we don't have the pressure to log it or do other high intensity uses," Adam says. "It's fun to take a property like this and steward it. Grapes have an amazing lifespan. They'll probably outlive me, which is kind of weird, but cool. If you do the right things, plant the right grapes, and have a sustainable business model, they should last 60 or 70 more years."

That would take Elk Cove into its second century of pioneering ways to gently extract value from Oregon's climate, soil and lifestyle. Like his parents, Adam is relaxed about the future of the family business. If there is one thing the Campbell story proves it is that patience and hard work pay off, however distant or unanticipated the result. "I don't want to put any pressure on the third generation," he chuckles. "But it will be great if they want to continue to steward the land and tend the vines that were planted so long ago."

For the Forest Grove Trail Guide turn to Page 206.

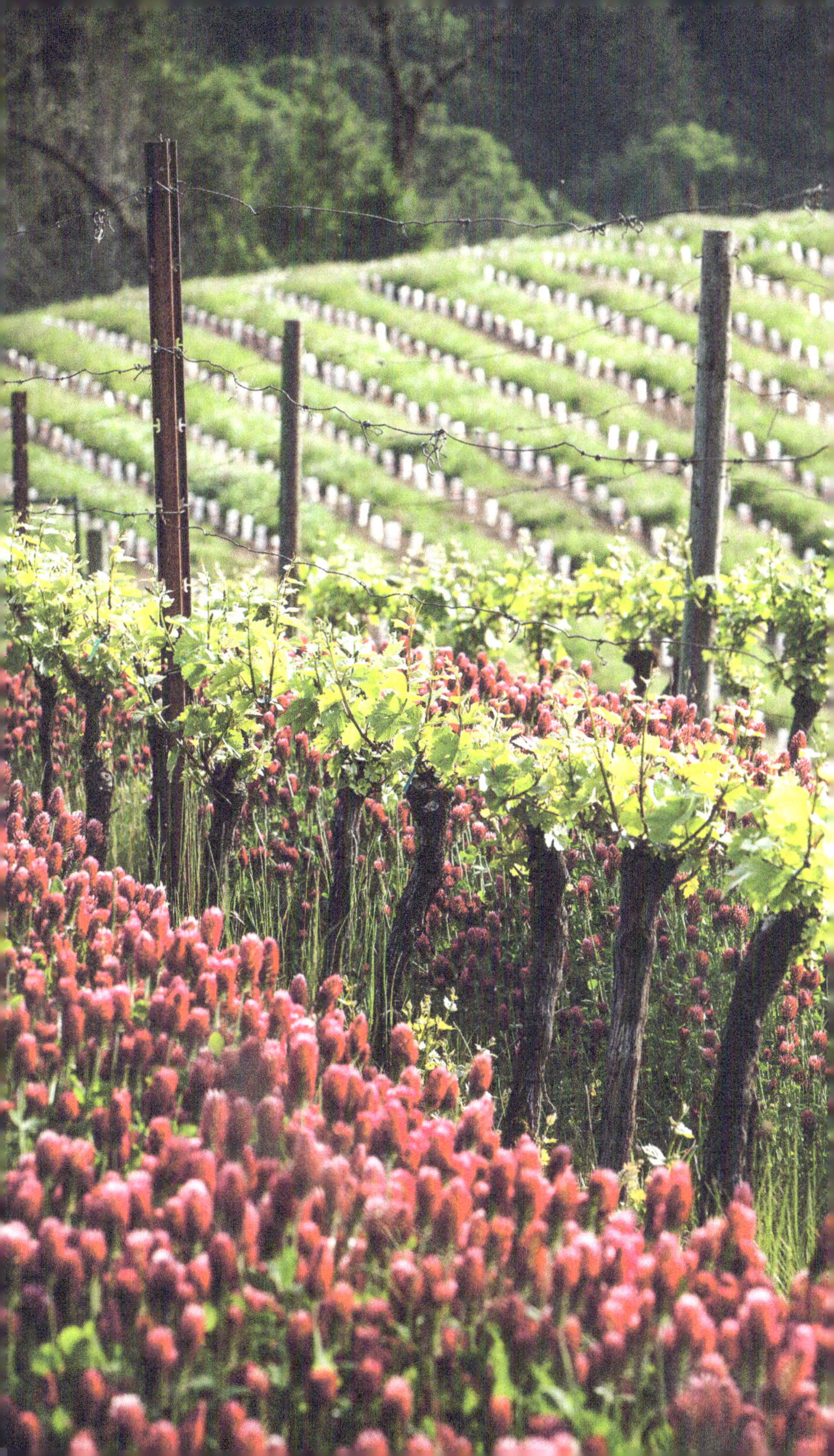

# Elk Cove Tasting Notes

**Elk Cove Pinot Noir Rosé**
Rose-petal pink. One-hundred percent Pinot Noir. Fresh strawberry and juicy grape.

**Elk Cove Riesling 2010**
Petrol nose. Apricot, lemon and lime, nice clean acidity.

**Elk Cove Riesling 2012**
Well-rounded white from the "best season in 50 years in Oregon". Ripe apricot and peach, vanilla notes, and subtle clover honey.

**Elk Cove Willamette Valley Pinot Noir 2012**
Lively ripe fruit, boysenberry, raspberry, and hint of cedar wood. This blend of grapes from its six vineyards is Elk Cove's most widely-distributed wine.

**Elk Cove Clay Court Pinot Noir 2012**
Deep ruby. Silken mouthfeel. Balanced tannins, blackberry and blackcurrant dominate with hints of clove and vanilla.

**Elk Cove La Boheme Pinot Noir 2012**
Elegant body. Ripe berry nose. Very smooth. Red fruit and currant with a hint of leather.

**Elk Cove Roosevelt Pinot Noir 2012**
Deep red almost Syrah color. Petrol nose. Beautifully smooth, new oak, concentrated ripe blackberry and raspberry, deep plum and hint of tobacco.

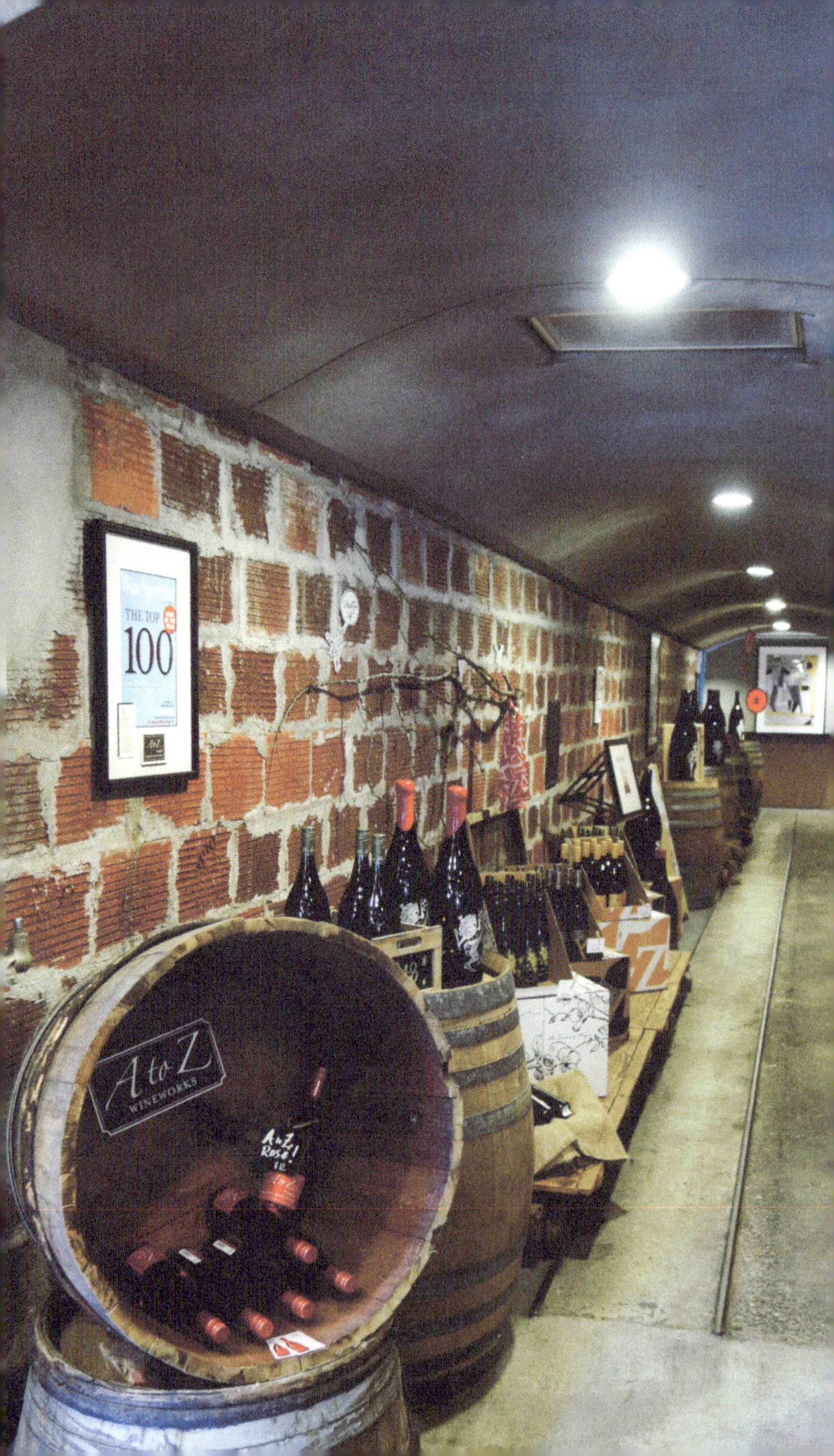
THE TOP
100
A to Z
WINEWORKS

# A to Z Wineworks

The doors glide open. I am suspended above a distant floor, staring into a room full of silver tanks the size and shape of missile silos. "This is my favourite part of the whole tour," says Carrie Kalscheuer, direct sales manager for A to Z Wineworks and Rex Hill. I'm not surprised. The fermentation hall looks like a Bond villain's lair. I scan the walls for countdown timers and glance up, half expecting to see the ceiling slide open.

Carrie is explaining what goes on in these giant cylinders: "A lot of people don't know the difference between how red and white wine are made. They don't even realize the inside of the grapes are the same and all the color comes from the skin. The whites we press out right away so there's no skin contact. We can put them in a larger vessel because they don't need to be pressed down or pumped over."

She pushes open another door and leads the way downstairs to the floor of the fermentation hall. As she continues her detailed, enthusiastic account of the technical aspects of winemaking I realize this is the epicentre of a plan for world domination – albeit a peaceful one.

In 2002 two couples – Deb and Bill Hatcher, and Cheryl Francis and Sam Tannahill – whose winery

## The Biodynamic Preparations (BD)

The preparations should not be seen as a substance but a force.

We use 9 preparations. The BD #500 and #501 are sprayed separately. The BD 502-507 are mixed together at the time of the compost preparation.

**BD #500:** Horn Manure - Stimulates root growth and humus formation. We usually spray at the beginning of fall.

**BD #501:** Horn Silica - Stimulates and regulates leaf growth. Usually sprayed in growing season just before or at bloom.

**BD #502:** Yarrow - Permits plants to attract trace elements in extremely dilute quantities.

**BD #503:** Chamomile - Stabilizes Nitrogen within the compost and increases soil life.

**BD #504:** Nettle - Stimulates soil health, providing plants with the individual nutrition components.

**BD #505:** Oak Bark - Provides healing forces in order to combat disease.

**BD #506:** Dandelion - Stimulates relation between Silica (S) and Potassium (K) so that Silica can attract cosmic forces to the soil.

**BD #507:** Valerian - Stimulates compost so that phosphorous components can be fully used by the soil.

**BD #508:** Horsetail - Prevents or controls diseases.

experience includes Eyrie, Domaine Drouhin, Archery Summit and Chehalem respectively, banded together, bought grapes and blended their own Pinot Noir. A little more than a decade later A to Z Wineworks is Oregon's biggest producer, making some 300,000 cases per year and shipping wine to every US state and 16 countries. They bought this property – the erstwhile Rex Hill vineyards, winery and tasting room – in 2007, and now produce about 10,000 cases per year of high-end wine under the Rex Hill label.

Outside, heavy machinery rumbles in the spring air. A to Z Wineworks is expanding to accommodate its ever-growing production. Inside, everything in the winery is as big, solid and chrome-y as a classic Cadillac. Leaving the cool fermentation room, we walk up a ramp guarded by yet another row of silver behemoths. "These are the blending tanks. A percentage of each fermentation goes into these to build the blend. They're the biggest tanks in Oregon: 34,972 gallons."

The number is so specific yet apparently arbitrary I have to ask, "Why?"

Carrie grins. "Because they are to the Nth degree the biggest thing you can put on the back of a semi-truck and take down Interstate 5."

Pedantic attention to detail permeates every aspect of A to Z Wineworks. Its industrial precision is

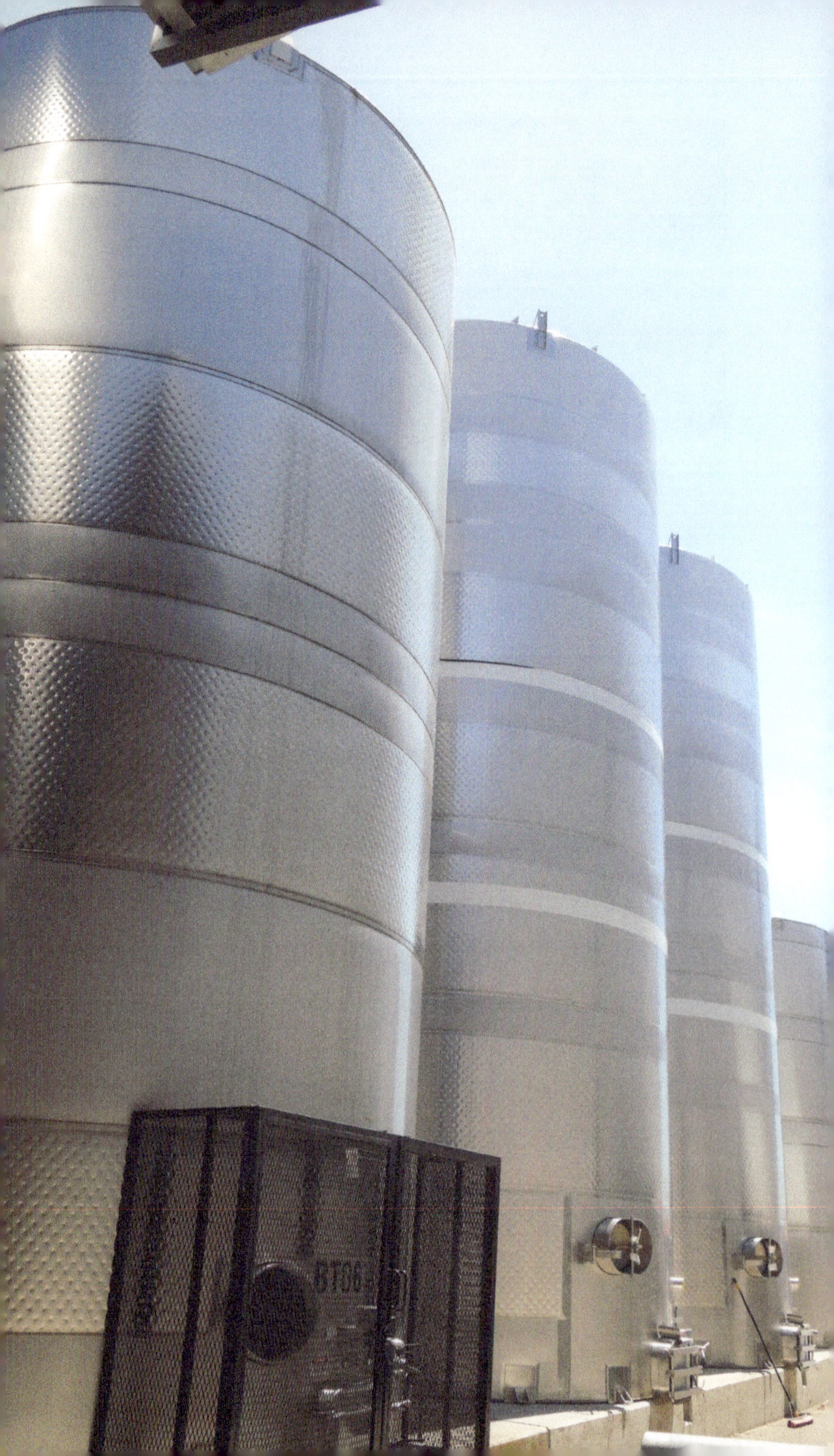

impressive but where are the earth-loving, fleece-wearing, back-to-nature Oregon vibes I've come to expect?

We amble past the mobile bottling line – which they use because it gives maximum precision and flexibility, ensuring every vintage is bottled at the optimum moment – towards a slope covered in luxuriant vines. Carrie apologises: "We just did a biodynamic spray so it smells a little funky."

Turns out that, Bond villain lair notwithstanding, all the vineyards A to Z Wineworks owns or long-leases are farmed biodynamically. Growing grapes based on the esoteric system designed by Austrian philosopher Rudolf Steiner seems an odd choice for a business so invested in technology and efficiency.

"There's a lot of hoodoo-voodoo that comes with it," Carrie admits. "It's difficult to understand how some of it works, but it definitely works."

She tells me they prune the vines based on the lunar cycle then segues into an analysis of the role of climate on their various vineyards. We're standing on the foothills of the Chehalem Mountains, whose 20 to 30 degree Fahrenheit diurnal temperature swing imparts certain qualities to its grapes, while the Eola-Amity Hills are influenced by coastal winds from the Van Duzer Corridor. Then Carrie veers back to biodynamics: "Deb, one of our founders, describes it like this: 'Organic is don't do anything bad to it; sustainable is leave it as you found it; and biodynamic is leave it better than you found it'."

A to Z Wineworks' zeal for improvement extends from its winemaking facilities and vineyards to its guests. Most tasting rooms are built to sell wine; A to Z/Rex Hill's is designed to immerse you in the sensory experience of wine. It is dominated by a vast round table covered in glass ramekins holding things like citrus peel, peppercorns, vanilla pods and cinnamon sticks. The idea, Carrie explains, is to introduce visitors to a broad range of flavor notes so when they taste the wine they have a vocabulary to describe what they are experiencing. Notably, the charming staff members are more like sommeliers than salespeople. This is, in part, because A to Z wine sells itself but mostly it's because they more interested in filling your brain than emptying your wallet.

"Education is our gig," Carrie says. "It's our best foot forward." She and the other trained sommeliers on staff teach classes and run tasting sessions for industry professionals and amateurs alike. "Our philosophy is to make wine approachable to everyone."

Technology. Precision. Biodynamics. Progress. Education. They're all fragments of a puzzle but there's a missing piece. A to Z Wineworks is too successful and sophisticated to have sprung from a philosophical grab-bag but I can't put my finger on what ties everything together.

"What do you want A to Z wines to say?"

Carrie doesn't hesitate – she never hesitates: "We consider A to Z to be the essence of Oregon. We harvest and source from all around Oregon and blend for that complexity Oregon can give us. You'll see 'The Essence of Oregon' on the bottles. That's our primary thing. Our mission is to craft the best possible wine we can at the best possible price."

"What defines 'best possible wine'?"

"Utmost quality. Anywhere else in the United States you only need 75% of a varietal to call it the varietal on the bottle. Oregon raised the bar and said it has to be 90%. You can't put the words 'Pinot Noir' on a bottle unless it's at least 90% Pinot. You can't hide anything."

She interrupts herself to introduce a woman who tries to slip past us towards the kitchen where the staff Cordon Bleu chef is making blueberry muffins. Co-owner Deb Hatcher doesn't look thrilled at the diversion.

"What are you writing?" she wants to know.

"Deb used to be an English professor," Carrie explains. "She's retained every bit of grammatical perfection."

At the mention of grammar Deb warms. It is clearly a favorite subject. She tells me that A to Z Wineworks is in the process of announcing its B Corp certification and she's keeping a sharp eye on the copywriter. "I don't like war terms. I don't like mechanised language. I don't like jargon. My husband Bill doesn't like sports analogies," she declares. "Shorter and clearer is better. We're careful about language. Not because we're trying to be jerks, or because I was an English teacher. We do it because if you stop and think about how you're going to say something you'll think about what you're going to say and be more present."

Deb explains that B Corp (the B is for "Benefit") is an association of over 900 companies around the world that work to promote environmental and social change. "The aim is to not just be the best in the world, but be the best for the world." Certification is not a vanity project: "You can't just decide to do B Corp. You're tested. You have to have a minimum score to qualify and do better every single year to keep your certification."

Then Deb is back to her favorite topic. "Language is about honesty, about integrity. If you start with how you think and speak then you're going to have integrity in your wine, in your business, in anything, really."

Voila. The missing piece. The link. The glue. I should have guessed. The clue is in the name: A to Z. You can say anything with 26 letters and this is a winery dedicated to expression. Climate, soil, elevation, varietals, and water, are the winemaker's alphabet. A to Z Wineworks uses them to tell the story of Oregon in the most gracious way possible: over a good glass of wine.

For the Newberg Trail Guide turn to Page 212.

# REX HILL WINERY

# A to Z Wineworks Tasting Notes

### 2011 Rex Hill Chardonnay

Tropical nose. Peachy with hints of honey and must. Lingering peach if you hold in your mouth. Smooth finish.

### A to Z Wineworks Pinot Noir 2012

Medium body and color. Red cherry and red fruit. Light spice and slightly tart. Smooth and inviting; a good introduction to Pinot.

### 2011 Rex Hill Vineyard Blend

Immediate punchy nose. Medium-deep color, medium body. Slight petrol nose and flavor. Blackcurrant and red cherry fruit. Juicy fruit to finish.

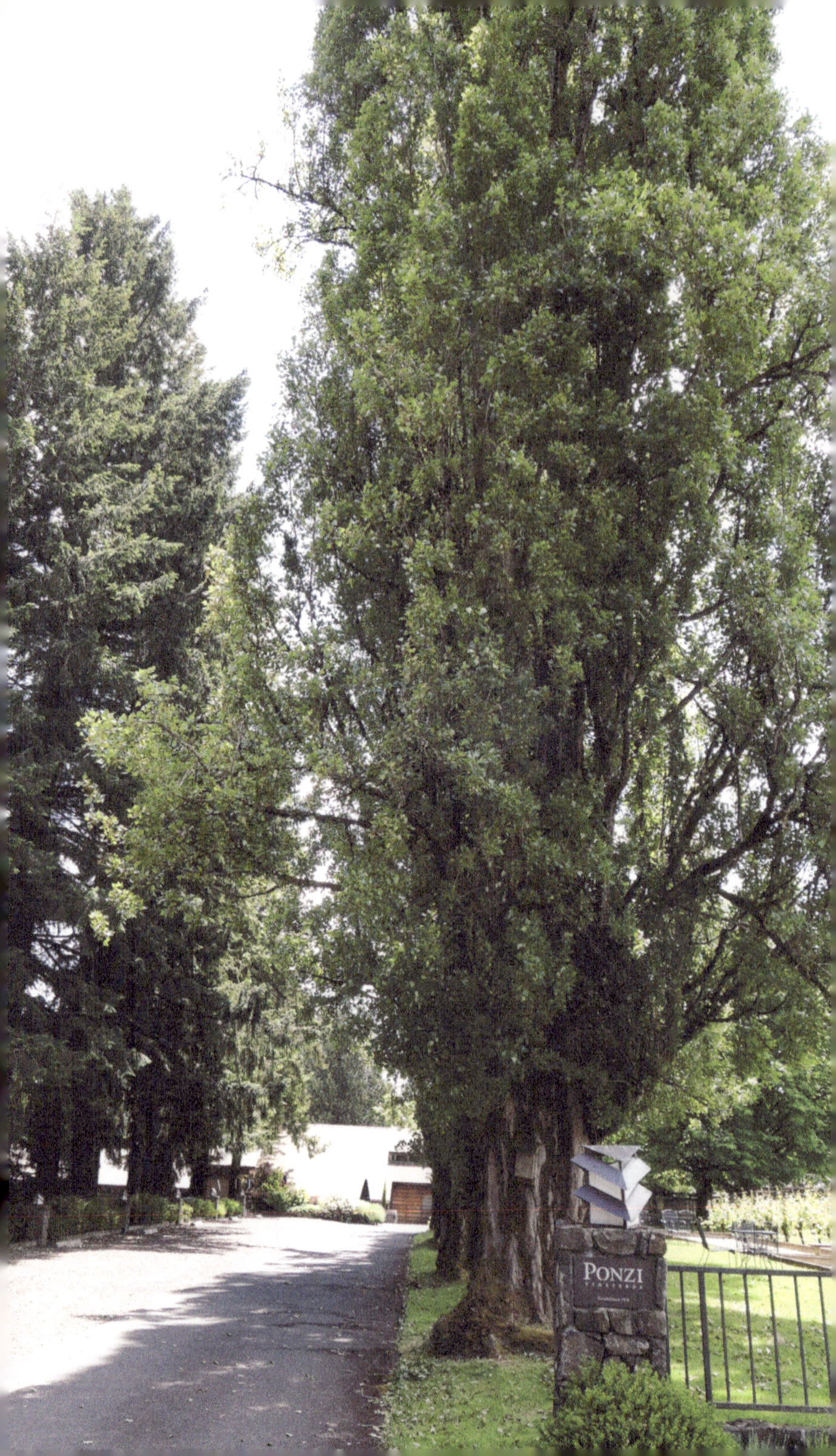
PONZI

# Ponzi

Spend any time in Willamette Valley wineries and you get used to a way of speaking. Winemakers, tasting room staff, even fellow visitors praise the land, the vines, the vintages. They repeat certain soothing words: climate, quality, community, collegiality. Looking out over the valley's pastoral beauty with a glass of $60-a-bottle Pinot Noir in hand you slip effortlessly into the argot of pride and positivity.

I am under the spell as I approach Ponzi's immaculate new winery and tasting room, an airy modernist building flanked by manicured lawn and pristine terraces. Eyeing this slice of chic structural perfection I can already imagine the fulsome phrases in store.

Winemaker Luisa Ponzi's huge, intelligent blue eyes crackle and pop with laughter: "Growing up on a vineyard was, from a kid's perspective, terrible." Her parents Dick and Nancy Ponzi planted their first vines in 1970 when Luisa was three years old. The wine-business was literally her whole life. "What my family was doing was embarrassing. Growing grapes and making wine was not something that was done in the Willamette Valley of the 1970s. My brother, sister and I were the labor force – working in the vineyards, the cellar, and tagging along to sell wine. We grew up, left, and thought we'd never look back. I definitely didn't want to be in the wine business!"

Her strong, scuffed hands rest briefly on the polished wood tabletop. We're tucked in a semi-private corner of the winery. Great sheets of glass are the only thing separating us from a panorama of vineyards and evergreen forests, intermittently shaded by cotton-candy clouds. It's hard to picture the virgin land. How much harder it must have been for the Ponzis to picture this.

"I don't know what made my parents think they could do it," Luisa says with a chuckle. "My father's an engineer. He's always trying new things, trying to figure things out. He loves to problem solve." Dick Ponzi had a successful career with Disney, engineering iconic rides like The Matterhorn and It's A Small World. "It wasn't as if he was running away from anything," his daughter notes. "But they were hippies, for sure, and wanted to get back to the land."

Home winemaking was a tradition in Dick's Italian family and he wanted to recreate that with his own children. He and Nancy travelled in Europe and fell in love with Pinot Noir. "That was the first part they got right," says Luisa. "They understood that Pinot was the right place to start, but they didn't have a grand vision of an industry. It was more personal: 'We want to do something new and different'. It was determination, interest and curiosity. They're huge risk takers."

Along with a handful of pioneers, including the Adelshiems and the Campbells of Elk Cove, the Ponzis helped form the Oregon Wine Growers Association, shaping a new industry guided by little more than idealism and a belief in Oregon's potential. Once a month they'd gather for potluck dinners. Afterwards, Luisa and the kids played while the grown-ups created structures and codes of practice, such as labelling laws and a self-imposed tax to fund research, that exist to this day. "Those dinners were fun," she admits. "The weirdness hit when I was a teenager."

Luisa finished high school eager to leave the "weirdness" behind. A life-long science buff, she got her college degree in biology and planned to study medicine. But a summer job at Oregon Health Sciences University, prior to medical school, quenched that desire: "I quickly saw it wasn't an environment where I would thrive." She was at a loose end when her father asked if she'd come work a vintage, "while she figured out her next step". Her parents had never pressured her to follow in their footsteps so she agreed, thinking the money would come in handy until she found something else.

"My dad was clever," she smiles. "He put me in the lab. For the first time I saw the science to winemaking. Growing up, it was all cold, dirty manual labor. Seeing the chemistry sparked my interest. I saw I could use my science background and be creative, where the medical field was not going to give me that creativity."

After several months in the winery, Luisa wanted to learn more about the science of winemaking. She considered UC Davis but – in a move her risk-taking parents no doubt approved – she went to study at Beaune in Burgundy. "I was the first American woman, in fact, one of the first Americans to ever go there." Armed with only high school French, she plunged into an 18-month course entirely in French. Despite the language challenge she thrived, honing her skills and palate, and earning a degree in enology and viticulture.

This sounds like a lot of work, considering she already had a job in the family winery, but surmounting obstacles is essential to the Ponzi ethos. "I knew a lot from working with my dad, so I didn't necessarily need the training but the credentials were important. It's hard to be the next generation. Your peers can say, 'it was handed to you'. I wanted respect. As second-generation, and especially as a woman, I needed to prove I was serious. That it wasn't just handed to me. I thought it was important and it was important, in terms of people taking me seriously."

Luisa is one of the pioneering women of Oregon wine. When she started her career the only other woman making wine in the valley was Lynn Penner-Ash, of Rex Hill and Penner-Ash. "She was my only mentor here," Luisa recalls. "There were a lot of wives behind the scenes. My mother worked hard – it was all hands on deck – but generally, women took a marketing or sales role. That's extremely important, obviously, but as far as the winemaker title, there weren't a lot of female role models." Though women remain a minority ("I still go to meetings where it's all guys, and me") Luisa says an increasing number of women are applying to work harvests and pursuing careers in winemaking.

She has succinct advice for aspiring enologists:

"Have a good base of scientific and academic knowledge but don't rely on that. You have to trust your intuition. The greatest winemakers in the world are the ones who are intuitive about winemaking."

Intuition sounds hippie and glib. Like, just feel the vines, dude. But Luisa has something specific in mind: "Intuition isn't something you're born with. You learn it. The problem is, you only learn one year at a time. Every vintage is different. Take 2013 – in the 20 years I've been doing this I'd never seen rain like that before. Intuition means trusting what you've learned in the past and figuring out how to apply it to what is in front of you. It takes a long time to get that confidence."

Time, along with climate and terroir, is a lead character in the story of the Oregon wine industry. Success beneath this wide sky calls for a particular attitude towards the ticking clock. Nancy and Dick Ponzi plowed their first acres knowing it would be years before they saw the outcome of their experiment. Even now, in a robust, rapidly growing industry, planting a vineyard is an act of faith. Great winemakers have to cultivate a patience modern life has bred out of most of us. "People are into experimentation here," Luisa says. "When you love what you do you constantly question and try new things. But it takes a long time to experiment. You start with an idea and don't see the fruition until two years later. Then you want to duplicate it to make sure it's real. You learn over five years, ten years."

For example: Ponzi's vineyards are on Laurelwood soil – a basalt base covered with younger freshwater sediment blown onto the hillsides after the Missoula floods. "Younger vines express sedimentary character. When the roots hit the fractured basalt they completely change. It's really cool," Luisa enthuses. "Depending on how high they are on the hillsides, and how deep the soil, it takes 15 to 20 years. At that point I see a shift from red, bright fruit to dark, brambly, tannic fruit and spice."

Most of us would find a 20-year wait for work results intolerable, but the stately pace of nature is a cherished part of Luisa's existence. "The best thing about my job is keeping in touch with agriculture. That is the starting point: watching the vines and the seasons. I love the fact the same things happen every year and you track your life by them." She devotes serious time to viticulture, collaborating closely with her vineyard manager of 15 years to cultivate the estate, which is LIVE certified and organically farmed. When she's not working harvest, or winemaking, she and her sister, Maria (who is president of the vineyard and co-owner, with Luisa, of the winery) hit the road to promote Ponzi and Oregon wine.

Luisa's scant spare time is spent with her husband, a fellow winemaker, and four children: travelling, growing a home vineyard, beekeeping, and tending an array of farm animals.

"What do your kids think of growing up on a vineyard?" I ask.

"It's so different. There's such pride. They love the fact we have a winery and make wine," She glances around the elegant, cathedral-like space, face alight. "They think it's cool."

For the Portland Trail Guide turn to Page 204.

# Ponzi Tasting Notes

**Ponzi Pinot Gris 2013**

Very pale – almost clear. Lemon nose. Floral, light peach and strong green apple. Clean finish.

**Ponzi Pinot Blanc 2013**

Medium body. Peach at the core with white floral notes, almost effervescent.

**Ponzi Arneis 2013**

A white Italian varietal thought to be extinct but revived from vines found in a monastery in the Piedmonte region. Honey nose. Rounded mouthfeel. Juicy apple, melon and grapefruit.

**Ponzi Aurora Chardonnay 2010**

Full mouthfeel. Refreshing minerality. Like biting into an almost-ripe peach with citrus notes.

**Ponzi Dolcetto 2012**

The name means "little sweet one" but it isn't actually that sweet. Medium body. Raspberry, strawberry and redcurrant with rounded tannins.

**Ponzi Pinot Noir Reserve 2011**

Deep color. Full body. Robust black cherry and dark fruits, rich spice with a hint of dark chocolate.

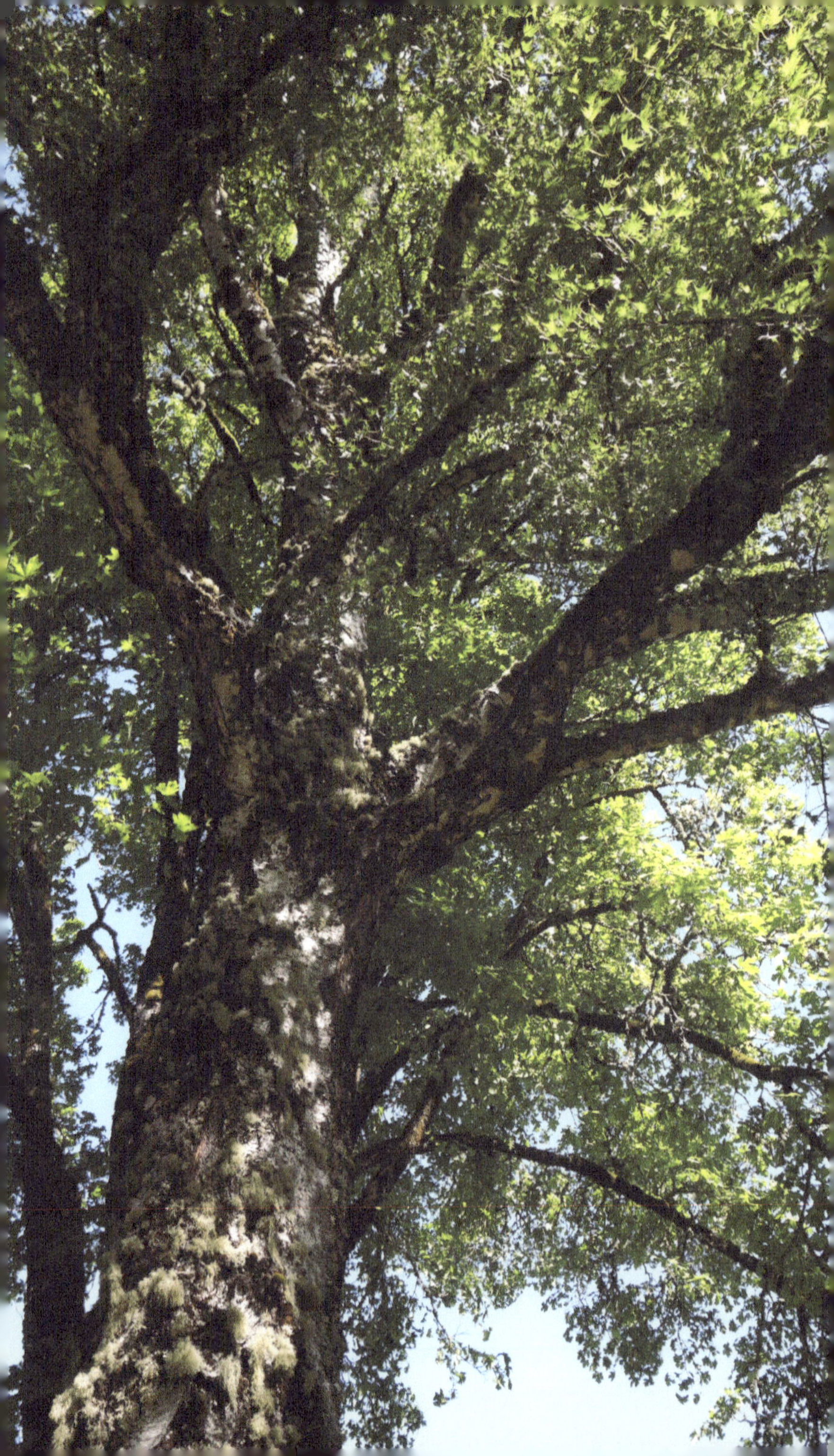

# Montinore

Rhododendrons, lilacs, roses, cypress, oak, and weeping willow channel the earth's exuberance into great bursts of foliage and color. The concrete walls of Montinore's winery and tasting room are lathered with brilliant green ivy. Chipmunks skitter on tree trunks, scolding the birds that loft saucily towards clouds hanging like puffs of whipped cream in the spring sky.

Inside is an anonymous, drafty basement office cluttered with standard business detritus: folders, plastic in-and-out trays, filing cabinets, and overfilled bookshelves. It could be a hardware store headquarters, or accountant's den, if it weren't for the books: *Wine and Food of Bulgaria*, *Winery Dogs*, *General Viticulture*, *Technology of Winemaking*, *Grand Vins*, a selection of wine atlases, and half-a-dozen brown binders stamped 'Oregon Pinot Camp'. Rudy Marchesi calls his dogs who come snuffling in and collapse beside his chair. "We're farmers, first and foremost," he says. "My responsibility is two-fold: to produce a high quality product. And to not only protect the environment, but to improve it. That's the work of a farmer." Hence the shelves freighted with books, the documents, the notes, the charts, the academic rigor invested in the fruitful land.

Born and raised on the East Coast, Rudy grew up

mucking around on his grandparents' farm in the Bronx.

Did I hear that right: A farm in the Bronx?

He nods. "It was a little slice of Eden. They had a quarter-acre with fruit trees, a vegetable garden, a wine cellar." As a seven-year-old he claimed a patch of ground and planted his first crops there. "The other thing, you know, was the stories of the old country. My family were farmers in Italy. They grew grapes and grains, they had animals. Our lore was agricultural. That stuck with me. It was very influential."

Nevertheless, Rudy set a course for a different life. He headed to Sonoma State University in California to study psychology. His family ties to California, however, were through grapes. During Prohibition his grandfather in the Bronx made wine to order for other immigrant families. He got the grapes from California.

"Prohibition wasn't really about wine," Rudy explains. "It was about controlling access to beer and spirits. After it started the government determined it couldn't stop people from buying grapes. So train-loads of grapes went east to New York, Philadelphia, and Boston for immigrants to make wine. The government left them alone because they were making it for themselves. I had an old neighbor who told me you could order a barrel of grape juice from California and by the time it got across on the railroad it had already fermented, so you had a barrel of wine." He chuckles: "Maybe of dubious quality, but it was a barrel of wine."

After the repeal of Prohibition his grandfather carried on making wine for his family, friends, and fellow Italian settlers. "They'd tell him what kind of wine they had in their region and he'd make something similar."

When Rudy arrived in California he bought enough Zinfandel to make a half-barrel then called his grandfather to ask what to do – "he walked me through it."

Despite his education in clinical psychology Rudy found the world of winemaking and vineyards irresistible. He settled back East and bought a small vineyard in the Delaware River Valley. He was operating the vineyard and working for a wine distributor when his daughter decided to attend Reed College in Portland in 1992. Trips to visit her turned into buying trips as he became familiar with local wine. "I realized Oregon had great potential, so I started taking wines back to the eastern market." Among them were vintages from Montinore. He developed a relationship with the then-owners. In 1998 they hired him as a consultant; in 2001 to oversee operations; then asked him to become president of the winery in 2003. In 2005, when they retired, Rudy bought Montinore.

"I get bored easily," he says with a smile, by way of explaining his radical reformation of the estate which had already seen major changes. At the start of the '80s the land was leased to a vegetable farmer. Then Mount St Helens erupted, dumping inches of volcanic ash over the Willamette Valley and putting the farmer out of business. The owners called in agricultural surveyors who said it was good vineyard ground and, in 1982, planted 360 acres of grapes. "They were very ambitious, but put the cart before the horse."

Oregon viticulture was in its infancy and the original owners didn't have a plan to market the wine. But they managed to get production running and, in 1990, built the winery where we're sitting. When Rudy bought the property he wanted to move the wine from "average" to excellent. "My approach was to start at ground level: to improve the quality of the vineyards, then move into the winery and change the way we produced the wine to dovetail with what the farm gave us."

He converted the farm from conventional to organic ("What people call 'conventional' only started in the 20th century," he notes. "People farmed organically for centuries before that"). This meant a labor-intensive process of replacing synthetic sprays with organic, planting cover crops, and starting a composting program. Rudy could have stopped there but, ever curious, he developed an interest in biodynamics. "I didn't really know much, but some of the great producers in France were doing it. If they thought it was better for their farm and made better wine, I wanted to know."

After taking a nine-month course in biodynamics Rudy chose two sub-par blocks as a test case. "On paper, they should have been great, but they weren't performing." The vines flourished under the new regime and – crucially – made better wine. In short order he started doing biodynamic sprays on 80 acres, within another year he'd converted the whole estate. Montinore is now Demeter certified biodynamic and Stellar certified organic, but is still a work in progress.

"I like fooling around with things," says Rudy, whose avocations include cheese-making, curing meats, and playing jazz guitar and piano. "It always sort of bugged me that you have all this space between the grapes so I'm experimenting. I have wheat growing, rye, barley, and triticale. Just this morning I tilled up a section to do some millet. I might not eat it, but I can feed it to my chickens."

He brings this same restless intellectual drive to all aspects of the wine business. For many years Motinore has been an active participant in Oregon Pinot Camp, a weekend in the country for 250-plus wine buyers from all over the country. This three-day event immerses buyers ("no press, no trade") in the unique qualities of Oregon wine in a very hands-on way. "We dig trenches in the vineyards to show them the soil type, we teach them about the different regions, show them how the wine is made." The fortunate attendees leave with a deep understanding of the characteristics of Oregon's fine wine, and an appreciation for the collegial spirit that helped form and continues to fuel the industry.

Willamette Valley winemakers' emphasis on education and collaboration was born of necessity: "Coming into Oregon there was a sense that something great could happen here. It was exciting. But we were the underdog, off in this top left corner of the country, by ourselves, so we had to work together to get any attention." Now, Oregon gets attention for all the right reasons. Montinore's Red Cap Pinot Noir 2012 was the only American wine to make a New York Times list of the ten best summer reds.

Montinore represents the great pioneer enterprise of melding Old World heritage with New World innovations and education to shape an ongoing tradition. Rudy's grandparents would be proud to see all he's accomplished. They would be even happier to know that his daughter Kristin is the estate's general manager – bringing the family lore that began on the distant hillsides of Italy to new life on the foothills of the Coastal Range.

For the Forest Grove Trail Guide turn to Page 206.

# Montinore Tasting Notes

**Montinore Almost Dry Riesling**

Smooth mouthfeel. Well-rounded body. Peach and green apple flavors with a hint of citrus.

**Montinore Gewürztraminer**

Straw color. Light body. Tropical fruit and vibrant citrus – lemon and grapefruit.

**Montinore Parsons Ridge Pinot Noir 2010**

Medium body. Lively acid. Ripe cherry and red fruits with notes of cedar wood and hint of cocoa.

**Montinore Pinot Noir 2012**

Deep color. Full body. Plum and black cherry fruit, moderate spice, vanilla and hint of smokiness.

GHOST HILL
CELLARS

# Ghost Hill Cellars

The beaten-metal 'Ghost Hill Cellars' sign is affixed to a lump of granite the size of an industrial freezer. It's the last thing Mike Bayliss's father would have imagined, or wanted, when he dynamited that hunk of stone out of a pasture a half-century or so back.

"My dad never made a mistake in his life," Mike drawls, dry as summer in the Sahara. "Other people caused things to go wrong, but he never did."

We're standing in the Ghost Hill Cellars tasting room, a chalet-roofed, wood-floor shack amidst a stand of towering oaks, set between a barn and the white clapboard farmhouse Mike's grandfather built in 1906 – the year he emigrated from Minnesota and bought the property. For most of the next 100 years the Bayliss family raised crops and livestock: beef and dairy cattle, sheep, wheat, oats, and hay. Then, in 1999, Mike planted six acres of Pinot Noir.

"We would have been one of the pioneers if we'd planted in the '70s," Mike notes. "But my dad thought it was a waste. He thought 'You don't need wine to survive. You need grain and meat.' He came from the Depression when if you didn't need it you didn't buy it."

Fortunately for Pinot Noir fans, Mike and Drenda see things differently.

Mike has been fascinated by wine since the '60s. When he and Drenda were dating he brought a jug of home-made sweet wine to share with her dad. They got through most of it before realizing the thick sediment on the bottom was in fact a layer of dead fruit flies. "He was mortified," his wife chuckles. "He didn't come back for a month." Despite the setback, Mike persisted with both wooing and winemaking. The couple wed in 1967. Over the years he took courses at Chemeketa, and spent time with Oregon wine legends like Don Letts and Ken Wright.

Years passed. Their son and daughter grew up bucking hay and raising steers for Future Farmers of America projects but time was running out for the land. "My dad used to call this Squirrel Hill, because the only thing it was good for was growing squirrels." But Mike had a notion the depleted earth could be put to better use: "People told us it was good grape ground."

"When Mike's dad was alive the land was worth little to nothing because of its poor soil," says Drenda. "But that poor soil makes it perfect vineyard ground."

The proof is a long wave of vines cresting the opposite hill, vibrant green beneath an enamel blue sky. They have 15 acres planted now. Half they sell and half goes to their winemaker Rebecca Pittock-Shouldis to make the 1200 cases that Ghost Hill Cellars releases each year. (I didn't have a chance to meet Rebecca and ask her about the path that led her from being a maintenance technician working on F-15 jet fighters to being one of Oregon's leading woman winemakers.) It's all Pinot because, Mike says, Pinot is the one varietal the Willamette

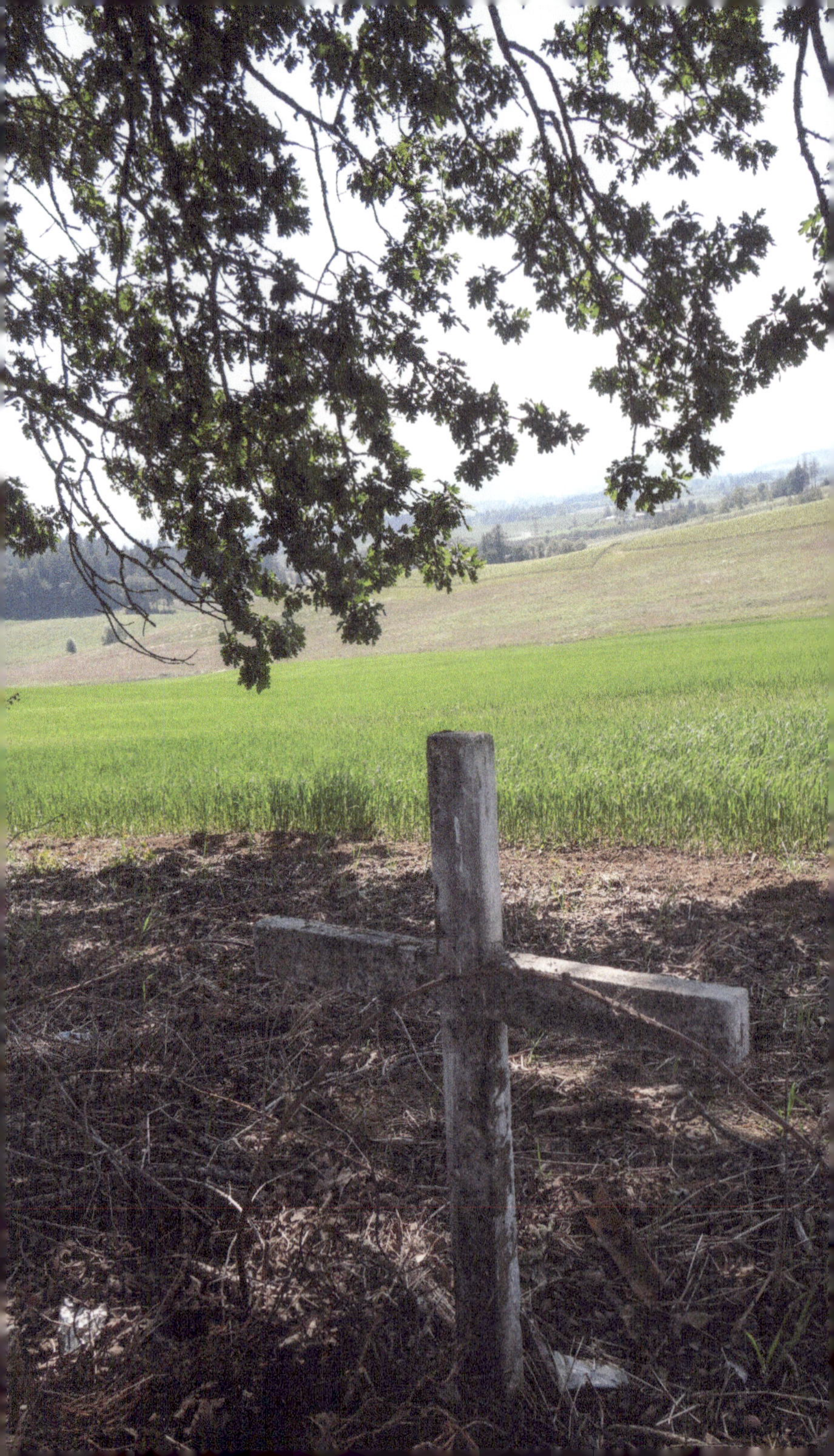

Valley grows better than anywhere else.

Pinot is a delicate grape; its wine a cultivated taste. Ghost Hill's refusal to compromise, or spread the risk, is probably a poor business decision on paper, but Mike has enough of his dad's flinty spirit to carry on regardless. The result? Multi-award-winning, world-class wine. We sample Pinot Noir Blanc, a white truffle of a beverage: rare, sophisticated and subtle. The Pinot rosé, which they make by leaving the skins on for 24 hours to bring out the color, is justifiably recommended by *Wine Spectator* as one of the world's best rosés. The 2010 Prospector's Reserve Pinot Noir silences me at the first sip. I want to climb into the bottle and savor every magnificent facet of this masterpiece. When Drenda and Mike urge me to take the rest of the tasting bottle home I feel as if I've been bequeathed a jewel.

Cultivating and crafting sublime Pinot Noir is their gift to wine-drinkers. In return the Bayliss's get a chance to pass their rural lifestyle and family traditions to another generation. Holding on to the land is a challenge all small farmers face in the 21st century. At 234 acres the Bayliss spread is too small to turn a profit in the era of industrial agriculture. For some 40 years Mike supplemented the farm income by working at the nearby Trappist monastery, doing everything from book-binding to building pews to baking fruitcakes.

"Planting the vineyard is about the preservation of the land in the family," Mike says in his wonderful, gargling-gravel voice. "There's nothing else I could have done that would have interested our kids and grandchildren in keeping the ground as part of their heritage."

Son Michael, daughter Bernadette and son-in-law Cameron Bower are partners in the business, each taking an active part. Michael – a mechanic for Ford – oversees equipment purchases; Bernadette and Cameron help with capital and plan to move back to Oregon in a few years to take a hands-on role; their nine-year-old son wants to be a winemaker. "We talk business once a week," says Mike. "It makes us closer than we would be otherwise."

As we walk outside to survey the vineyard Mike points out pieces of history. The chunk of gleaming amber stone is fire opal, "probably washed down from the Missoula floods in Montana". On the step below, half of a worn stone bowl, an Indian artifact his father found in a field – perhaps while traipsing behind the horse-drawn plow whose rusting blade rests against a tree stump. Among other relics, they recently discovered a couple bottles of moonshine stashed in the barn.

"We didn't open them, but maybe we should," Drenda grins. "They look okay."

Mike explains that during Prohibition some of the farm's grain output went into bootleg whiskey. "Dad and the neighbor ran a still. The neighbor had a milk route. It worked out well: a couple of milk bottles and something to go with it!"

I clamber into his Ford Super Duty pick-up and we cruise towards the vineyard. Mike points out a massive live oak at the peak of the hill to our right. "If you stop up there on your way out you'll see the cross I put under the tree," he says. "Oak Springs Farm Road is part of an old military road that ran from Washington to California. One night in the late 1800s a miner camped there. During the night he was murdered for his poke of gold and his horse was killed. Since then, he's been seen astride his horse, looking for the one who took his life and his gold. That's why it's known as Ghost Hill."

When we hit the middle of the vineyard we get out and venture down the rows. The Willamette Valley unfurls like an emerald carpet dotted with dark stands of oak and hemmed by distant, deep-blue ridges. It is splendid to be outside in air as fresh as clean laundry, watching birds of prey loop lazily in the distance. Perhaps one of them is the bald eagle that nests on the farm. There is an abundance of other birds, bees and butterflies, too. In its previous incarnations the farm was heavily plowed and sprayed. Mike and Drenda stopped that, reducing inputs to a minimum and leaving the ground intact. Now the land is once again a haven for flying things, plus a loud, lively population of tree-frogs. Ghost Hill Cellars is sustainably farmed and LIVE and Salmon Safe certified.

Back in the tasting room, Drenda confesses she never expected to be a farmer's wife. Her parents moved

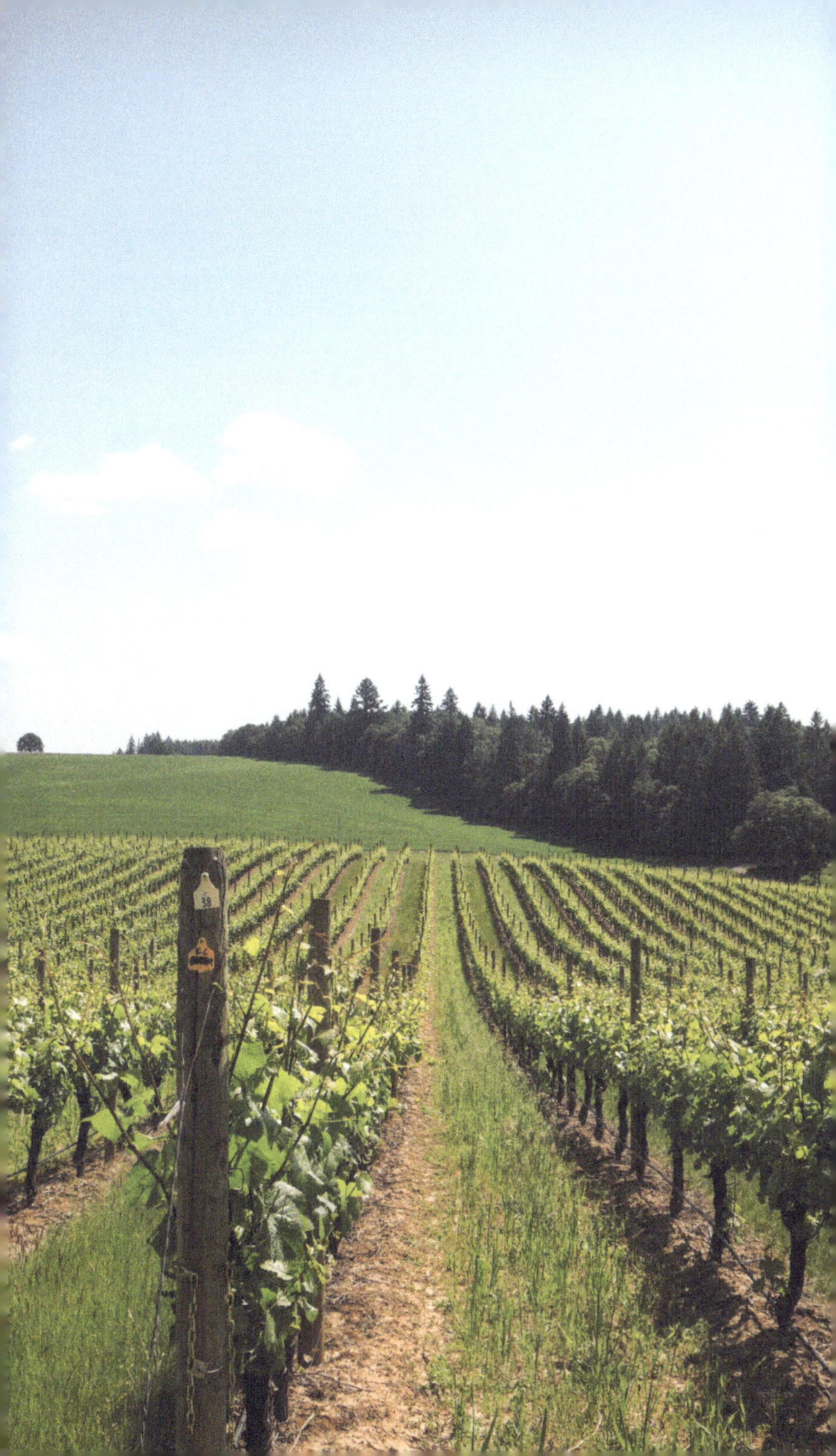

to McMinnville when she was a senior in high school. "I hated them for it. We had been living five miles from Disneyland then all of a sudden I'm in this little town where people still drove horse-drawn buggies." One day, on her walk home from school, a young man offered her a lift in his '66 Pontiac GTO. She said yes. "I wouldn't have gone for a buggy." Abandoning her plans to return to California, Drenda married Mike and embarked on a life of hand-rearing rejected calves, chasing spooked cattle down highways and innumerable late nights baling hay.

Grapes, she says as an aside, are a lot more manageable than cows.

"They're not going to run," her husband deadpans. "You pretty much wake up in the morning knowing where they are."

Not that running a vineyard is easy. Pinot is high-maintenance and the couple work hard with their vineyard manager to keep the vines in perfect condition. There are other unexpected obstacles. A fire broke out at Scott Paul winery where they produce their wine. They raced there, along with five fire trucks, and watched flames shoot out of the roof. "We thought, that's it, it's gone," Drenda recalls. But amazingly, the fire spared their wine. "Luckily we'd just bottled our rosé and blanc. Otherwise they would have been ruined."

Vagary and mercy are implacable facts of life. Plans change, land gets weary, technology demands more production for profit. Equally: fate smiles, poor soil grows magnificent fruit, ghosts rest in peace. You can fight change or embrace it. Mike and Drenda chose the latter. Their family and Willamette Valley wine alike are better off for it.

For the McMinnville Trail Guide turn to Page 218.

# Ghost Hill Cellars Tasting Notes

**Pinot Noir Blanc 2012**

Pale rose gold color. This oak-aged white is full-flavored. Smooth tropical fruit, peach, and a hint of vanilla.

**Spirit of Pinot Noir Rosé 2013**

Bright berry nose. Medium bodied, slightly acidic. Tastes of strawberry jam with raspberry and red cherry notes.

**Bayliss-Bower Pinot Noir 2010**

Medium color. Petrol nose. Smooth, delicious, spicy, black fruit. Elegant hints of oak, cherry and vanilla. Opens to reveal juicy raspberry and boysenberry.

**Prospector's Reserve Pinot Noir 2010**

One of my favorite Pinots. Medium body. Rounded blackberry nose. Spicy, zingy cherry fruit, hint of raisin. Sublime, a wine I'd be happy to serve or drink any time.

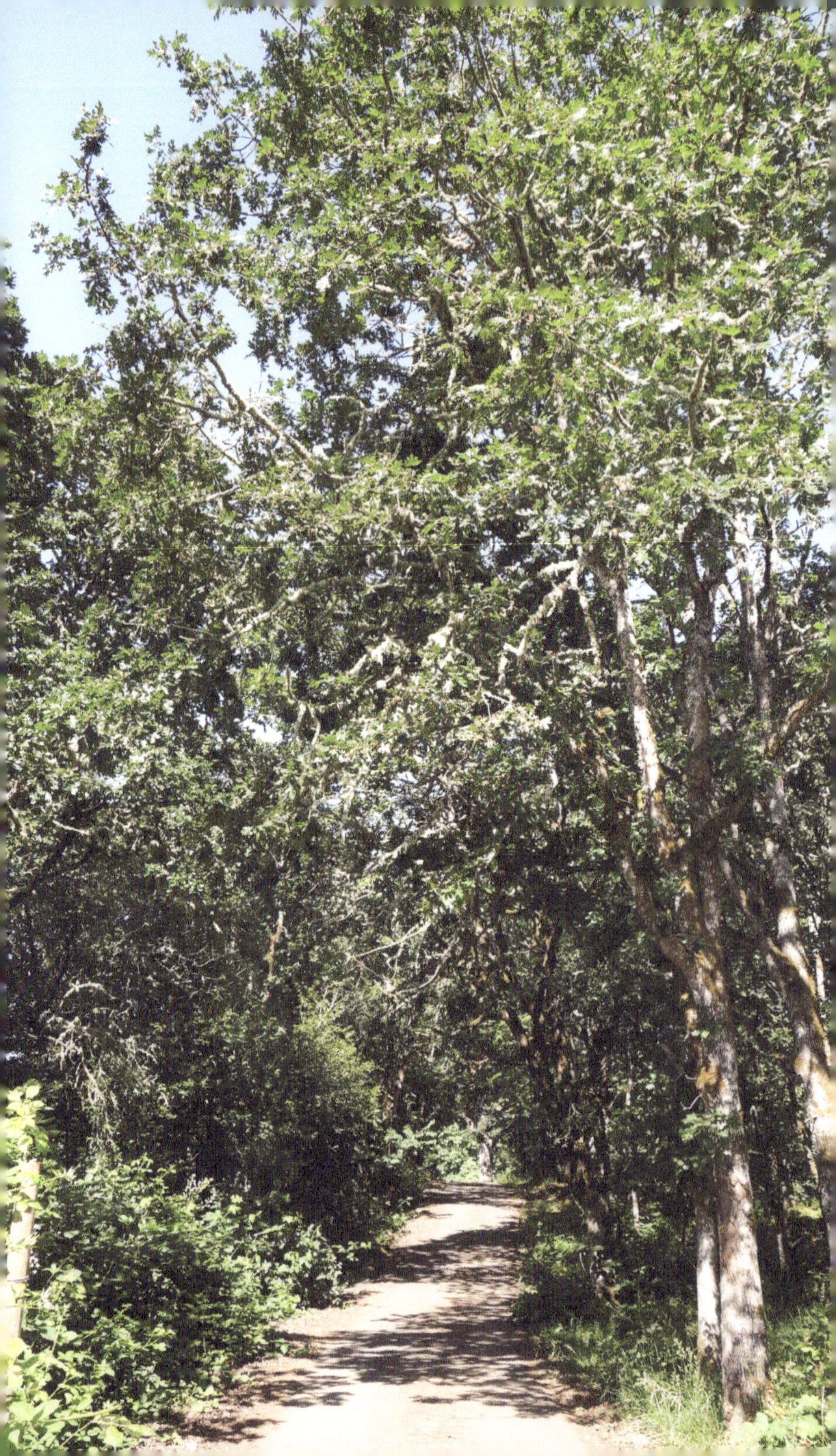

# Whistling Dog Cellars

Whistling Dog Cellars co-owner, winemaker and viticulturist Tom Symonette places a gnarled finger on the vine: "Typically three buds break at each node. We'll pull off one or two to leave one strong shoot growing."

My boot heels sink in the dirt as I scribble, notebook balanced on my forearm, face warmed by the ascending sun. A quarter of an hour ago I turned at a battered black mailbox and found myself in a tunnel of resplendent oaks. A lifelong Robin Hood fan, I half expected a troupe of merry men to appear amongst the trees. Inching through the filtered green light I came to a little red barn set in a field of red, yellow, pink and white poppies, bachelor's buttons, and snapdragons, and hemmed by moss-swathed oak and breeze-stirred fir. Just beyond, the gravel track opened onto a vineyard – its outlines fuzzed by early morning mist. Tom greeted me and a moment later I was swept into a stream of information about grapes and viticulture, facts flowing fast and imperturbable as a river.

Tom knows to the inch where each of his vines were grafted onto the rootstock, which clones are where, how deep the clay topsoil is, the height of the fruiting wire, and a hundred other details. His conversation is peppered with references to stomates, inflorescences, $CO_2$, crop density, nitrates, spacing, and trellising. At first, it is hard to believe this man spent most of his life amid suits and spreadsheets in Silicon Valley. But as we mosey along the rows, pausing to scan the sky for the kestrels that nest in vineyard's bird boxes, a picture emerges of a man whose life – like the vines he tends with such intense affection – had three buds. Two of which, removed, left one strong shoot.

"It's kind of a strange story," Tom says, revealing a streak of Midwestern modesty when the topic turns from plants to his personal life. Born in the Bahamas, he moved to Iowa with his mother after his parents divorced. He grew up in the heartland and, at his mother's insistence, went to college. Unable to settle on a major he skimmed through disparate courses (political science, pre-vet) then dropped out and went to work in forestry. This sparked his interest and he went back to college to get a Bachelors and then a Masters in forestry. He graduated during the Reagan administration, which slashed federal land management budgets. Tom couldn't find a job. "That was the end of that," he says. One bud, pulled away.

Tom went back to school to earn an MBA, then went to work in corporate finance. "Not stocks and bonds. The running-the-company part." It was a professional life that was long on financial reward but short on satisfaction. He worked 100-hour weeks for businesses that would bloom, flourish and bust in the space of a few years. "I got sick of it," he says simply. "In finance you work on spreadsheets, you email them to someone, maybe they do something with them, maybe they don't. That's it. The most tangible thing you do is print out a spreadsheet." Finally Tom and his wife Celeste, who works in the pharmaceutical industry, decided it was time to change their lives. "Our dream was to work for ourselves, to live in the country, to be able to survive on that." So he quit the world of finance; there was one bud left.

One thing I hear over and over in the Willamette Valley is how the smallest things shape the largest futures. How a childhood memory or experience can, like a railway switch, alter the direction of a whole life. Tom's switching point was a high school foreign exchange trip to France. The teenage boy from Iowa was fascinated by his host family's habit of leisurely lunches. "The father would come home. His wife would put out a big meal and everything would stop for two hours. Of course, wine is a food in France. Every day we had white wine, we had red wine. I just enjoyed wine since then."

Tom started making wine as a hobby during his corporate career in California. When he decided to leave finance he went to Fresno State University to study enology and viticulture. "Fresno is known for emphasizing the practical aspects of winemaking. They have a commercial winery, which all the students work at, and before you graduate you manage a portion of the vineyard for a year, doing all the agricultural activities." This hands-on training clearly played a role in Tom's approach to winemaking but I suspect the source of his encyclopedic knowledge lies deeper. Anyone can take a course, absorb information, follow directions; but only a few digest what they learn and transform it into something distinctive.

By the time he approached winemaking as a profession Tom was drawing on a full life. The influence of the spreadsheet years is plain in his absolute attention to numeric detail: heights, weights, angles, dates. Subtler, though perhaps more significant, is his patience. He is comfortable with the fact that things don't always go to plan. If it weren't for budget cuts by the federal government in the '80s Tom might be a forester. The patience and application he learned in his previous work plays a vital role in his approach to wine.

"My philosophy is to do all the intervention in the vineyard. There are lots of practices – particularly on a small scale – that affect the quality of the grapes. That's where I put my work. One month of the year is winery work. The whole rest of the year, seven days a week, is vineyard work."

Ten of Whistling Dog's 16 acres date back to '81-'82, making them some of the oldest vines in the area, which is part of the Eola-Amity Hills American Viticultural Area (AVA). The original layout was 12-foot spacing between rows, six to eight feet between vines, and a single high-wire trellis. This was the dominant practice at the time, based on two things: what worked in California and equipment constraints. Most agricultural machinery, Tom explains, is designed for field-crop agriculture. Viticulturists had to plant rows broad enough to fit US tractors or go to the expense and hassle of trying to import equipment from Europe. Usually, it was easier to go big.

Tom is in the process of increasing the density of these acres, planting rows between the old vines to reshape the vineyard on an Old World model. This isn't nostalgia though: it's good science. He calculated the amount of sunlight the rows receive, changed the trellising, determined when to pluck the leaves so the grapes get optimum sun exposure. "We do our manipulation in the vineyard rather than the winery. I know lots of winemaking tricks but my goal is to not use them, to let the wine make itself and show what Oregon has to offer."

Like all the incomers I meet, Tom and Celeste are enthusiastic Oregonians. "I wanted to make Pinot and there are only a few places in the world that make top quality Pinot right now. It came down to New Zealand or Oregon.

"A friend and I visited about 30 vineyards around here, talking to winemakers. I thought, This is nice. The attitude, the way people act, their lifestyle, their standards, it's a lot like the Midwest. I liked that. I brought my wife and she loved it. We never made it to New Zealand."

What the Eola-Amity Hills lack in rugged Antipodean splendor they make up for in pastoral abundance. We trek down the road to the red building I passed earlier: Whistling Dog's spanking new winery. The air is warm with a hint of a breeze. Bees tumble through the flowers – honey and bumble alike – providing a humming undercurrent to the bird choirs chanting across the clearing. A trio of vultures trace lazy circles above us, scanning the field for a mid-morning snack. I feel like an extra in a tourist board ad. Scenery doesn't get lusher, prettier, or more quintessentially Oregon than this.

Tom made his first few vintages at neighboring St. Innocent Winery before investing in this deceptively quaint building. He points out the $30,000 press that gets used 24 hours in the year, along with other high-priced gear that gives rise to the joke that the quickest way to make a million in the wine business is to start with two. "The vineyard is beyond break-even but the winery is losing money," he says frankly. "But this is something I really want to do." He places six tulip-like Pinot glasses on a barrel and starts opening bottles. "What is most satisfying is knowing I did this. My work is right here. It's good wine. People may buy it or not, but it's tangible. I'm proud to have something to show for my work."

Tom pours the 2010 Heritage Blocks Pinot. He can, and does, explain how the year's weather contributed to its medium hue and hints of camphor, redcurrant and unripe cherry. For a minute though, I succumb to the pleasure of drinking instead of writing. It is a Coco Chanel of a Pinot – chic, lean, timeless as a little black dress. Like any legitimate work of art, the wine expresses its creator's philosophy, effort, joys and disappointments. Right there, in the bottle is proof that everything you cut away contributes to the beauty and complexity of what remains.

For the Salem Trail Guide turn to Page 222.

# Whistling Dog Cellars Tasting Notes

### Whistling Dog Cellars Dijon Blocks Pinot Noirs

**2010** - Medium color and body. Acidic. Bright fruit – primarily cherry and raspberry. Tingles on the tongue, rewardingly complex.

**2011** - Lean, mineral, flinty, acidic. redcurrant at first, plum and prune on the midrange, unripe blackberry. A cold, wet year.

**2012** - Deep ruby color. Petrol nose. Medium acidity. Bright red cherry fruit with notes of red plum and prune.

### Whistling Dog Cellars Estate Blocks Pinot Noirs

**2010** - Medium-light color. Petrol nose. redcurrant and unripe cherry fruit, hint of camphor. Delicious, chic, lean, acidic, love this wine.

**2011** - Fuller bodied than the 2010. Red berry nose. Ripe red cherry and red berries with vanilla notes.

**2012** - Deep ruby. Full body. Surprisingly acidic. Spicy blackberry and black cherry nose. Ripe berries with a hint of sandalwood and vanilla.

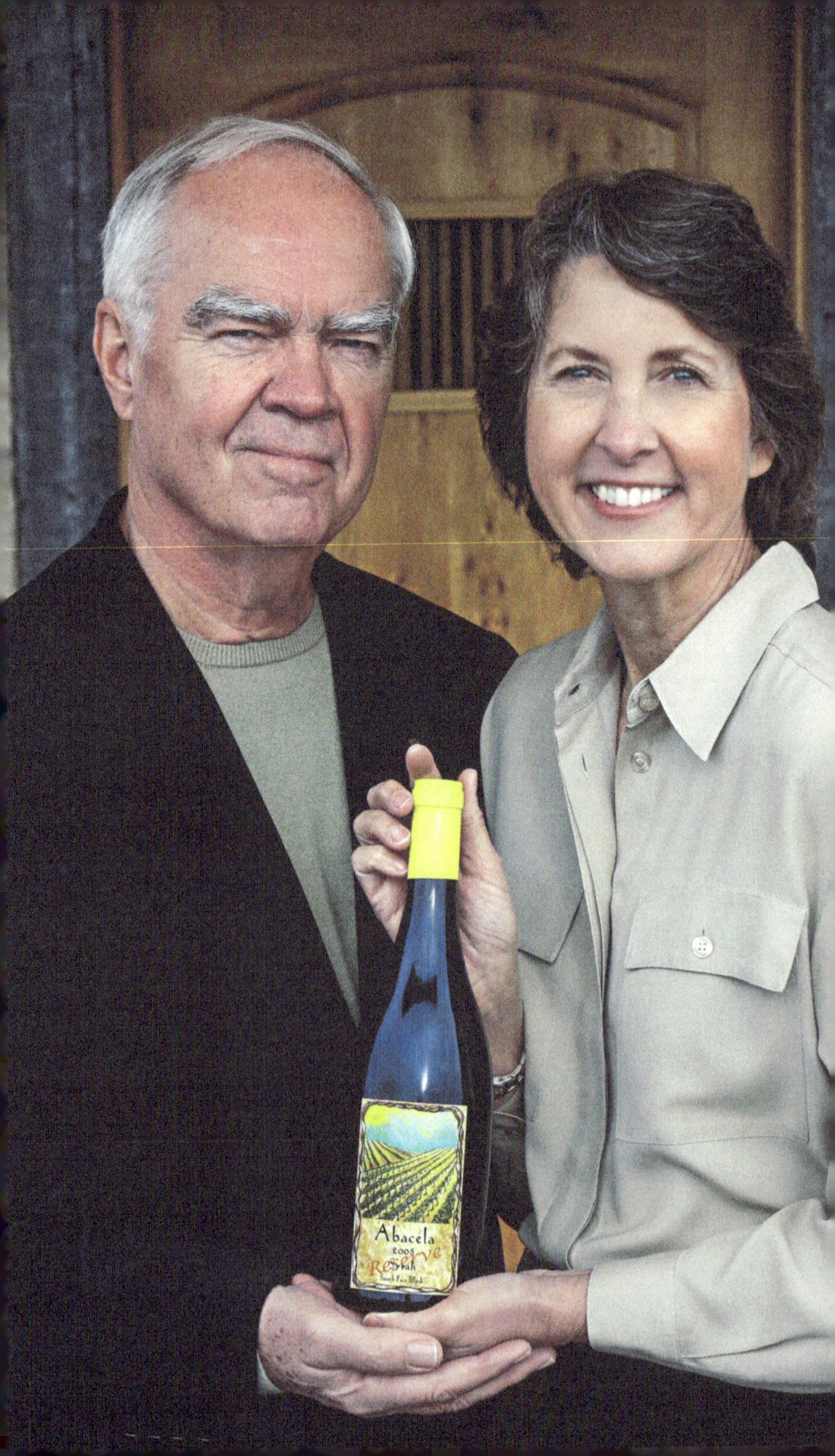
Abacela
2005
Syrah
Reserve
South Face Block

# Abacela

Abacela owner Earl Jones remembers his first taste of fine wine with a clarity most people reserve for marriage proposals: "I was sitting on the third table from the front in Commander's Palace in New Orleans, on the second floor, on the Saint Charles side of the building." His dinner companion was an insurance salesman trying to close a deal with the medical student. Between them, a bottle of Pouilly-Fuissé. "I thought, 'Holy cow, this is good!'" Earl left the restaurant insured to the hilt and enamoured of wine.

Fast-forward a few decades: Earl and his wife Hilda are proprietors of *Wine Press Northwest's* Best Winery of 2013. Their vintages win awards by the fistful. They pioneered varietal Tempranillo – Spain's classic grape – not just in Oregon but in the United States. It's an unlikely trail for a Midwestern farm boy to blaze, but that's what pioneers do.

Earl was born in Michigan, raised in extreme Western Kentucky across the river from Illinois, and Missouri. His parents grew row crops: corn, soybeans, wheat, oats. "We weren't drinkers," he notes. "We weren't sophisticated people." Once a year, at Thanksgiving, he was allowed a dram of whisky. With no desire to farm, Earl set his sights on science. He got an MD from Tulane University and became a researcher in immunology. It was in California, during a ten-year stint working at UC San Francisco that he learned about Spanish wine: "The best wines were Rioja. I thought Rioja must be a great grape," he chuckles. "I had no idea."

He relates this tale as we study a sign on the grounds of Abacela's sprawling Spanish villa-style winery. It looks like one of those roadside historical markers but instead of pointing out a rare bird or defunct trading post it is covered in graphs illustrating the climatic differences between Bordeaux, Napa Valley, and where we're standing in southern Oregon's Umpqua Valley. The story of Abacela is in these details.

Earl worked out that Rioja was a place and that the grape he so enjoyed was Tempranillo. A researcher to the bone, he had more questions: what made his favourite wine great? Was it soil, climate, a winemaker's magic touch, or some combination thereof? California grew Tempranillo but used it to make jug wine. What was the secret of his beloved Spanish vintages?

Ask how his quixotic, two-decade quest for an answer grew into the solid reality of an 80-acre vineyard producing extraordinary Tempranillo, along with other varietals including Syrah, Albariño, Grenache, Malbec and Viognier, and Earl drops into a professorial cadence, parcelling out information so you can take notes.

It took four things, he says. First, his farming background. "How many immunologists in America know how to drive a tractor? That was an advantage."

The second advantage was his research career, which meant trips to Europe that gave him a chance to taste fine wine. Next: his curiosity, which prompted him to keep asking the question even though he never got a satisfactory answer. The final piece of the puzzle was a sea-change in the medical profession. He found the rise of HMOs and the resulting restrictions on medical discretion "morally reprehensible" and decided to get out of medicine.

He was in his 50s, with a young family to support, wondering: "What was I going to do with the rest of my life?" His criteria for the next move was simple but strict: "Something similar to scientific research. Something I would never conquer. Something that would challenge me forever." Growing grapes was an option but lots of people did that. "Then I found out that nobody had made Tempranillo as a fine varietal wine in America." It was a "great moment" made even better by the fact viticulturists told him it couldn't be done.

Delighted to have found a mountain nobody had climbed, as he puts it, and convinced that all he had to do to pioneer great Tempranillo was find its elusive quality factor, Earl headed to Spain to do research. He visited wineries and received familiar, inconclusive answers about soil, climate and winemaking wiles. Undaunted by his lack of Spanish language skills, he grabbed a dictionary and dug up climate data. "I discovered the climates in Rioja and Ribiera del Duero, where they made the finest wines, were virtually identical – and very different from Spanish regions where Tempranillo made only ordinary wine. Eureka! All I had to do was find that climate in America and most of my work was done."

His matter-of-fact Midwestern delivery belies the fact that he was the first person in 150 years of US winemaking history to puzzle this out. Ask how it felt to crack the Tempranillo climate code and Earl's voice slows to a syrupy drawl: "I feel good about it, down in the cockles of my heart. How many times in life can a person have an original thought, something that no one has ever thought about before?"

The only thing rarer than original thought is, perhaps, the courage to act on it. "One of the criteria for doing a harebrained thing like starting a winery is you have to be a romantic idealist," Earl says. "And you got one here." Other criteria include determination and being willing to follow where the dream leads. Earl was still teaching when he had his "Eureka!" moment so, after poring over climate data and pinpointing specifics like frosts, prevailing winds, latitude (which determines daylight hours) and diurnal temperature shifts, he used lecture trips to scout possible vineyard locations in Idaho, Colorado, New Mexico, Arizona, Washington, and California. But the closest match was Oregon. Then, it was an educated guess. They almost bought property in the Rogue Valley but he reckoned the frost risk was too high. An undeveloped stretch of scrub oak savannah at the southern end of the Umpqua Valley, however, looked just right. "We wanted to buy some land, the owners were willing to sell some, so we planted some grapes."

Earl makes it sound as if everything fell like dominoes. But the Jones family spent years running on hard work and hope. When Earl's farmer father came to visit he took one look at the property and said, "Son, you lost your damned mind."

Earl's boy Gregory wanted to know, "What if you fail? What if you can't grow grapes? What if you can't make wine? You've never faced anything like this before."

"I told him: 'You only have to face things like that if you plan to fail, and I don't plan to.'"

Gregory came round to the wine business. He is now a professor at Southern Oregon University and a world-renowned expert on climate structure and suitability for viticulture, and how climate variability and change influence vine growth, wine production and quality.

Armed with how-to books and his tractor-driving prowess ("It's like riding a bike"), Earl, Hilda and their younger children threw themselves into creating a vineyard. Their daughter Hanna was 12 at the time.

She remembers recruiting friends to spend eight-hour days helping to plant grapes. "Mom was doing the books and running the tasting room. Dad was on a tractor for 15 hours a day. My little sister Meredith was four. She played in the mud all day. I was the field labour," Hanna says with a smile.

Meredith grew up to be an invaluable vineyard worker and crew manager before following her parents' footsteps into science. Hanna, an artist and designer, drew the original Abacela logo when she was a girl. It captured the feel of the vineyard so well it remains their emblem. Years later, after becoming an interior designer, she returned home to shape the elegant winery. "I worked on the layout, the rooms, the materials, the orientation, everything. It was a labour of love." Affection colors her voice: "I'm so proud. My parents created something from nothing. I hope I got some of Dad's tenacity – it's a rare quality."

Tenacity saw them through many challenges, like the year birds gobbled most of the ripe crop ("I cried," Earl admits); coping with a too-small winery; and being dragged out of bed by the phone on Saturday and Sunday mornings to sell wine

"Nobody told me you had to sell wine," he remarks wryly. The learning curve was short and steep: they would trek to Portland with samples and, after restaurant buyers were suitably wowed by a taste of Tempranillo, break the news it was from Oregon, not Spain. The restaurants would order a case or two, customers would ask where it came from, and the Joneses would get early morning calls from strangers wanting more Abacela wine.

Abacela's second commercial vintage, the '98 Estate Tempranillo (which Earl made using a book and his intuition), beat 19 Spanish entries to win a double gold medal in the 2000 San Francisco International Wine Competition. It was the first of many medals, but what the man who left his parent's farm "never wanting to grow anything again" prizes most is the fact his father, who passed away in 2001, "lived to help us pick and help us make the wine, that he saw the success."

"How did that make you feel?"

Tears glint in his blue eyes: "Wonderful," he murmurs. "Just wonderful."

From the corn fields of Kentucky to the vineyards of Oregon, Abacela's singular success proves there is no question so obscure, no task so demanding, no dream so fantastic that it lies beyond the reach of courage, intelligence, tenacity and whole-hearted passion.

For the Abacela Trail Guide turn to Page 228.

# Abacela Tasting Notes

**Abacela Tempranillo Barrel Select 2011**

Deep color. Medium-full body. Rich blackberry and dark fruit laced with spice and dark mocha undertone. Complex with a long finish.

**Abacela Syrah Estate Barrel Select 2011**

Dark ruby red. Rounded body. Intense black cherries and blackberries with peppery notes and slight nuttiness.

**Abacela Vintner's Blend #14**

Signature blend of Tempranillo and 13 other varietals. Smooth, full mouthfeel. Ripe fresh fruit and darker notes of plum and spice.

**Abacela Albariño 2013**

Classic Spanish white. Bright acid. Crisp green apple, pear and mango with a slightly creamy finish to soften its clean mineral edge.

**Abacela Port 2012**

Deep garnet color. Full body. Rich blackberry, plum, fig and spice with a hint of cocoa with balanced sweetness. Extraordinary Oregon take on ruby port.

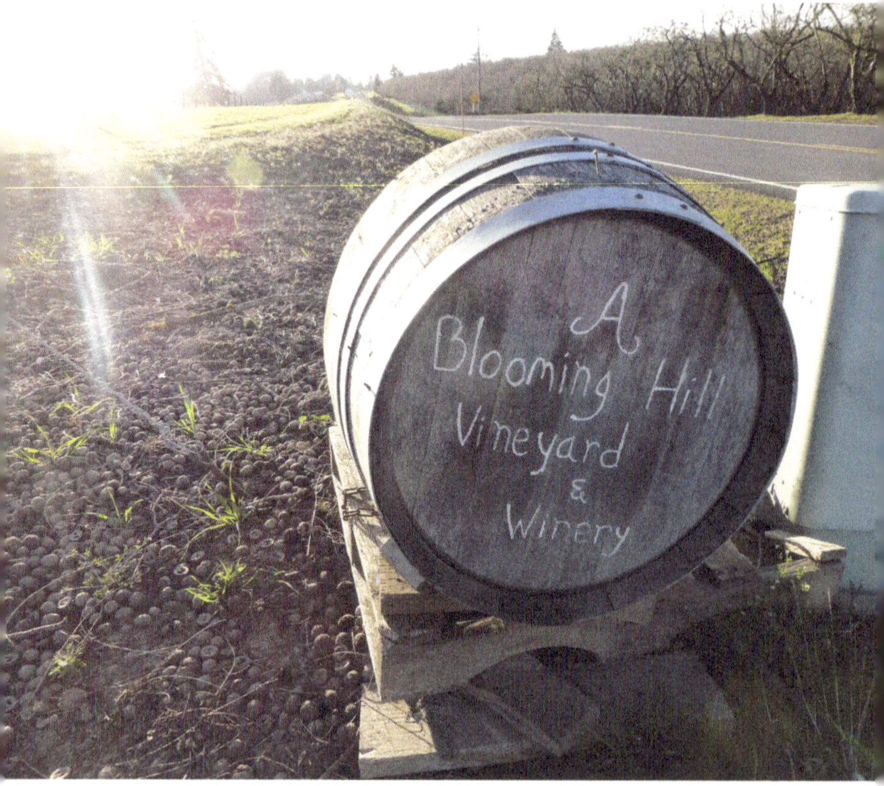
A
Blooming Hill
Vineyard
&
Winery

# A Blooming Hill Vineyard

"It was like Mad Men," Holly Witte says with a smile, recalling the era when she and her husband Jim Witte first met. It was the 1960s. He was a TV producer working with stars like Barbara Streisand, Merv Griffin and the denizens of Sesame Street. She was fresh out of college. Jim's wife hired Holly to be his secretary. It wasn't an office affair though, not like that.

After this brief working acquaintance their lives diverged. Holly fell in love with and married one of Jim's colleagues. They had a child and, when she was widowed in 1980, Holly built a successful career in fundraising and brought up her son. Eventually she moved to Seattle. Jim continued producing and filming TV shows and live events. He even had a brief rock'n'roll moment managing Kiss. He and his wife Marilyn lived in New York, with a stint in Hollywood. Many years later, nearing retirement, they moved to Portland.

On a brilliant April morning A Blooming Hill Vineyard's name is self-explanatory. I shift into second to follow the curves of the narrow asphalt strip rising with the swell of the Chehalem Mountains. Dense ranks of ancient evergreens rise on the left. To the right, burst after burst of color: pink, fuchsia, white, coral and yellow rhododendrons, azaleas, and irises overlook the sweeping slope of the vineyard. The dogs greet me first: Gemini, whose buttercream fur sloughs off in my hands, and Trouble, a pit bull mix with a head like a battering ram. Holly is close behind, waving hello, bobbed auburn hair bright in the sun, a fine gold chain around her neck. She leads me through a thicket of flowers, pointing out apple trees shading a wicker swing, an Asian pear, a plum tree. Sweet spumes of wisteria cascade over the railing of the deck. "Do you want some cuttings?" she asks, hopeful. "We have so much."

    We pass an empty niche where St Francis of Assisi stood until he was martyred by wood termites. To its left is a bronze bird-bath; beyond, another profusion of plants half-obscuring a wooden gazebo they call a Tea House. The tasting room is technically their basement but its view over forest and vineyard, and the surrounding abundance of plants and flowers, make it feel like an intimate British country pub. Trouble follows, almond eyes fixed on Holly as she selects bottles of wine. Jim comes in, iron grey hair freshly slicked. His hands are work-worn; eyes intense blue.

Jim's fascination with grapes and wine began in the basement of his granddad's Michigan farmhouse, sixty-odd years ago. "My grandfather, who I truly loved, liked making wine. He'd draw it out of the barrel into an Early Times bottle and say, 'you can have a drink Jimmy, but don't tell grandma'."

Those early happy memories stayed with Jim through his years in the world of television. His gift for making great TV meant he could buy a farm in upstate New York and escape Manhattan to spend weekends planting, growing and planning. He still had a dream to fulfil though: he wanted to own a vineyard. California was one option but by the time Jim approached retirement prime vineyard land was too expensive. He called a friend in Oregon and their discussion lit on the Willamette Valley.

"Will-uh-met" Jim enunciates, grinning.

His friend corrected him: "It's Will-am-ett, dammit."

Once he got the pronunciation right Jim found

the A Blooming Hill Vineyard property and took a TV job in Portland to smooth the transition from coast to coast. He retired not long after and threw himself into planting vineyards and bringing his boyhood dream to life.

The other half of the story, meanwhile, unfolded in their personal lives. Holly was living in Seattle with a long-term partner. Jim's wife Marilyn passed away in 2004 after a long illness. Holly's boyfriend died about the same time. An old mutual friend suggested they meet up.

"Larry said, 'it's so close, you should really have lunch'," Holly recalls. "Jim sent me directions but didn't tell me how long it would take. Four hours later I got out of the car thinking, 'where the heck am I?'"

Jim barbecued a salmon. They picnicked by the pond and drank a nice bottle of wine. Holly went back to Seattle.

When Jim called she said they could be friends but he was "geographically undesirable".

On May 20, 2006 they wed in the Tea House which Jim built for the occasion, surrounded by blooming hills.

Two years later, they entered wine from their first commercial vintage in the annual Pinot Noir Shootout in California. It won Silver in a field of over 400 Pinots from around the world.

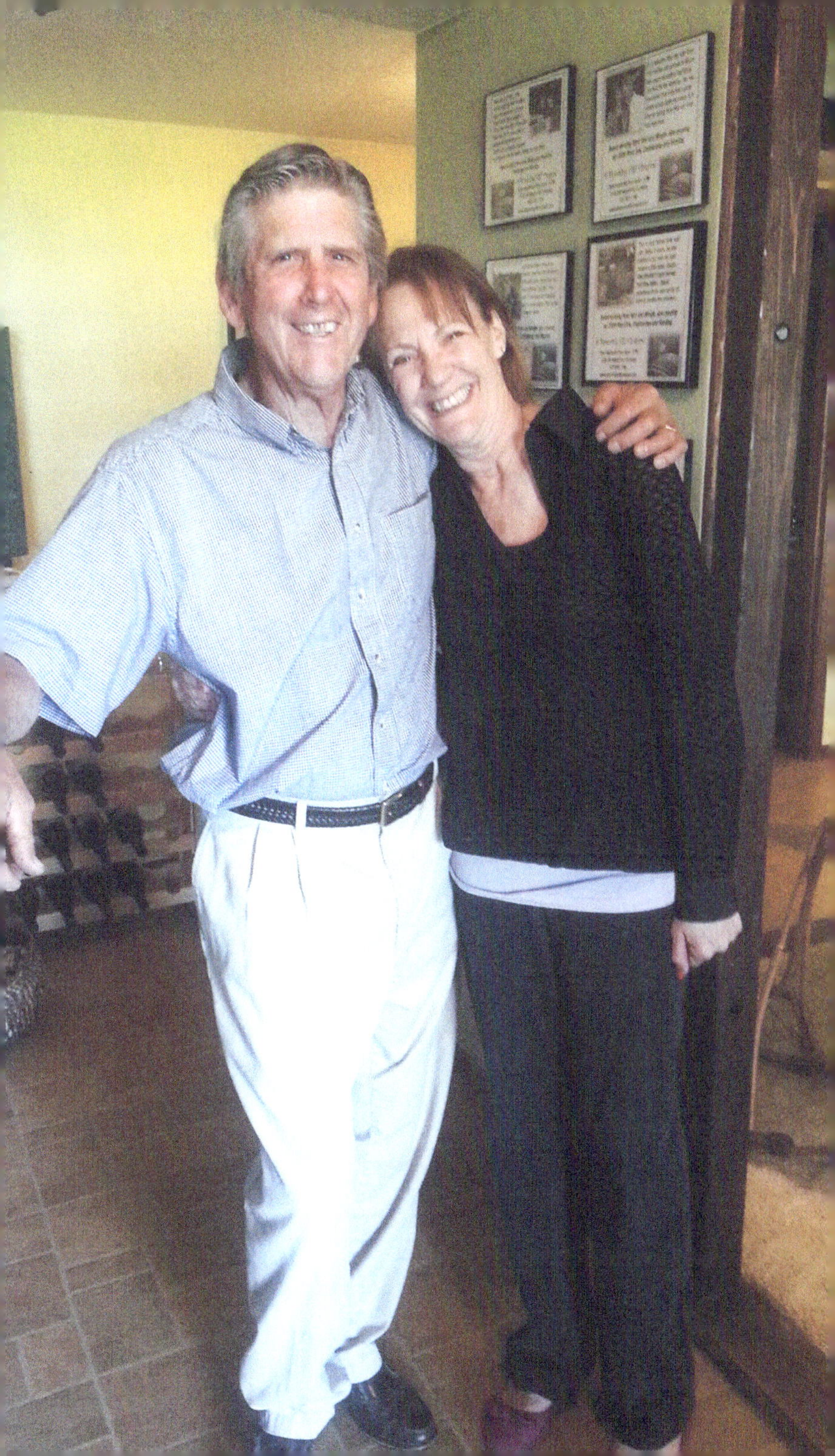

"Scared the heck out of us," says Holly.

"I thought, 'hey, this is easy'," says Jim.

They talk like they're dancing: a step, a turn, back, forth, but always in harmony, flowing in a way two can and one can't. They radiate contentment and mutual delight, making it hard to imagine the scene any different. But it wasn't always happily ever after. Not so long ago they were bereft, separate, each nothing more to the other than a name and a distant memory.

"This is a dream," Holly says, "but you have to shape that dream."

You have to get up in the morning to plant, water, prune and tend. You have to drive four hours for lunch. You have to keep calling, even if you're geographically undesirable. You have to leave your home, work and friends to move to farm country and get married. You have to take chances, in other words. You have to risk it, have to start without knowing the outcome, have to push on even when it's hard or sad or people think you're crazy for trying.

Because you don't know until you do how good it could be.

"It's a glorious thing to do," Holly says, looking around at her domain. "The land is unmistakably beautiful and the tasting room is like having a little salon."

For Jim, the thrill is bringing his ideas to life:

"I've always liked building things: a house, a farm, a television business, a winery. It's just enjoyable." As well as planting the vineyard he put in pastures, hayfields, barns and arenas for their herd of quarter horses and thoroughbreds.

"It's not a retirement at all," Holly notes, a twinkle in her eye. While Jim focuses on the outdoor labor, she masterminds the sales and market development. One of her projects is Sip 47, an association of local artisan producers and winemakers, all of whom are dotted along a 20-mile stretch of Hwy 47. It includes SakéOne, Oregon's only saké brewery; Bull Run Cider; Kookoolan Farms & World Meadery; plus a host of neighboring wineries. Weekends she opens the tasting room to share the fruits of A Blooming Hill Vineyard.

"We get groups who come in grumpy but they

leave laughing," says Jim. "It's not because of the alcohol. It's because they enjoyed themselves, they had a break in a tough day, or a difficult week."

"It's a way for people to connect," Holly adds. "We just give them a lovely time."

The tangible pleasure of the wine grows from their respect for the land and traditional winemaking. Jim uses natural sprays and techniques such as planting trees to stop erosion. One of the unique things about A Blooming Hill Vineyard wine is its low sulphite content. Holly used to get hives when she drank wine due to a sulphite allergy. But Jim uses very little of the preservative, say 100ppm versus 350ppm in some wines. "That was the magic sign," she smiles. The wines includes Mingle, a white blend of Pinot Gris, Riesling and Chardonnay; and a Port-style wine VXX (the numerals are their wedding date: 5/20) in addition to their Pinots Noirs.

"Isn't it interesting the wines are so different?" Jim muses. "They're all the same grape, from the same place, but it's the big guy up there saying, 'this year we'll do it this way.' You can't fight nature. You just follow his lead."

"It amazes me that Oregon Pinots have the reputation they have," Holly chimes in. "They're different from vintage to vintage, vineyard to vineyard, but overall they have that quality." She reckons it's to do with the "perfect" land and the Oregon attitude: "The collegiality of the people who decided to make wine here is a big part of it. Everybody wanted to help everybody else. What's good for you is good for me, and is good for all of us. The wines get better year after year."

Her husband picks up the thread: "Oregon is the

new melting pot. Holly's from Brooklyn via Seattle. I'm from Chicago by way of New York and Hollywood. There are people who've been here forever, the 100-year-old farms, then a whole, huge influx of new people. "

"What are your core values?" I ask.

He chuckles: "When the day is over we cook dinner together and have a bottle of wine. That's our core value. We talk about what she did and accomplished, and what I did. We talk about the future."

"We say, 'it was a successful day. We got through.'"

Jim and Holly share a smile. Gemini barks to be let in. I remember the opening line of Langston Hughes's poem 'Harlem': "What happens to a dream deferred?" Sometimes – with patience, love and hard work – it comes true.

For the Forest Grove Trail Guide turn to Page 206.

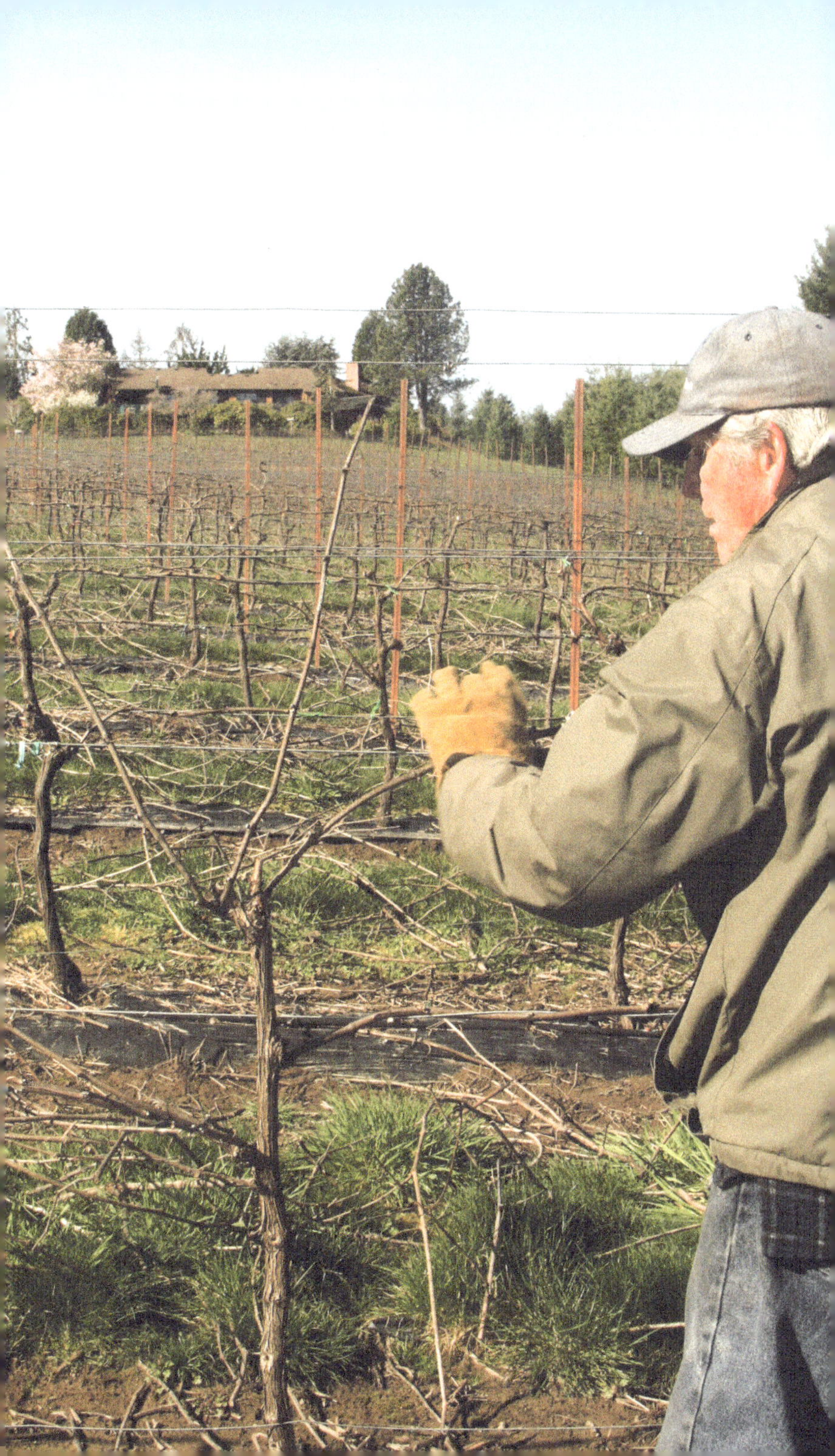

# A Blooming Hill Vinyard Tasting Notes

### A Blooming Hill Vineyard Mingle
Signature white blend of Pinot Gris, Riesling, and Chardonnay. Crisp, light, citrus with floral notes.

### A Blooming Hill Vineyard Riesling
Soft mouthfeel. Peach with a hint of vanilla, medium sweet.

### A Blooming Hill Vineyard Pinot Noir Blush
Slightly acidic. Light strawberry fruit, touch of redcurrant – like a not-quite-ripe fruit salad; tastes of spring.

### A Blooming Hill Vineyard Pinot Noir 2010
Jammy nose. Blackberry, black cherry with a hint of pepper, medium tannins.

### A Blooming Hill Vineyard VXX
Port-style wine made from pure Pinot Noir. Raisin nose. Mellow mouthfeel. Sweet. Complex dark berry flavors. Lingering note of dried dark fruit.

ILLAHE
VINEYARDS

# Illahe

Typewriters are by no means rare in Oregon. The Smith-Corona in the Illahe office is not, however, a hipster accessory. Nor is the chalkboard where someone has scrawled: "Buy more chalk". Or the phonograph and four-foot high wooden speakers bookending crates of classic rock LPs in the corner of the warehouse. National sales manager Bethany Ford hunts for seating: "We had folding chairs, but Brad didn't like 'em."

She can poke fun at Illahe's winemaker because he's also her husband (they met working at a winery). Her father-in-law Lowell Ford, who co-owns the vineyard with wife Pauline, helps her squeeze scavenged non-folding chairs into the cramped office which – in addition to typewriter, chalkboard, books and papers – is cluttered with beakers, coiled glass tubes, pipettes, unfamiliar mechanical contraptions, glasses and bottles. The single small window gives a view of gunmetal clouds. Lowell and Bethany chat about their new horses, a team of Norwegian Fjords.

They already own Percherons, a breed of French draft horse. "We wanted smaller horses to mow with," says Bethany. "We were going to get one but I found this team. If you find a team that was trained together it's pretty bad horse manners to separate them."

"They're brothers," Lowell adds, "and they're just devoted to each other."

Family matters at Illahe. As does quality, craft, and individualism.

There is something characteristically, stubbornly Oregonian about the way three generations of Fords (counting Brad and Bethany's young son, who helps Granddad Lowell drive the tractor) draw deep from the well of the past to nourish the future of Willamette Valley wine.

Before you jump to any hasty conclusions, it's Brad who is the driving force behind Illahe's embrace of traditional methods. His father Lowell is as responsible as anyone for the modernisation of Oregon's wine industry, thanks to his work founding the Northwest Viticulture Center at Chemeketa Community College in Salem. A grape grower since the early '80s, Lowell suggested the course to his colleagues after he officially retired from his job as the college's Dean of Students in 1998. They agreed to give it a try and the course was soon so over-subscribed they had to hire more instructors. "The students were really interested," Lowell says modestly. "A lot people in my class went on to establish vineyards and wineries." (Chemeketa alumni I meet include the proprietors of A Blooming Hill Vineyard, Björnson and

Plum Hill.)

Brad, an aspiring writer with a Master's degree in classics, followed in his father's footsteps at Chemekta. First as a teacher, then as a student.

"He surprised me," Lowell says of his son. "He was a grants writer and teaching poetry part-time. He said 'I'm bored to death'."

Talk turned to Brad getting involved in the 80-acre vineyard Lowell bought as a retirement project and named Illahe – Chinook 'earth'.

"I told Brad to go back to college because he didn't know chemistry." So he did, taking classes at Chemeketa and Portland State University.

"Brad has a real brain for chemistry," Bethany beams. "He took organic chem at PSU and got the best grade in the class."

There is still no sign of Brad in the flesh – he's somewhere in the warehouse – but his wife and father's refulgent pride intrigues me. Bethany talks about the peddle-powered pump he built for transferring wine into the barrels. Lowell speaks fondly of his son pitching in to build a pole barn. Buying horses was Brad's idea, as was their 1899 Pinot Noir made using strictly pre-industrial methods. "1899 never touched dry ice, canned nitrogen, enzymes, stainless steel, forklifts, packaged yeast, electric pumps, or filters," reads the website's description. Bethany adds that Brad turned off the warehouse lights and lit candles to rack the barrels. It's easy to guess who's behind the record player and LP collection. What motivates him? What do these deliberate anachronisms signify?

Bethany pours Illahe's sold-out 2012 Bon Sauvage Pinot Noir, a spicy wine with a cherry and licorice nose and a mouthfeel like oiled silk. "This is all-native fermentation. Instead of adding packaged yeast we let the vats ferment on their own," she explains. "It's how they used to do it in Burgundy. Native yeasts are risky. They can cause a lot of spoilage but they also create a really interesting wine."

Brad finally sidles into the office, looking like he'd rather be elsewhere.

"We were talking about you," Bethany smiles.

"I hear you're really good at chemistry."

He shoots me a sharp, blue-eyed glance from behind thick glasses: "It's not too hard to memorize little molecules."

Lowell already mentioned Brad helping in the family's old vineyard as a kid, so I try again: "But you grew up knowing about wine?"

"A little bit, uh huh. Not a lot."

Bethany steers the conversation. Brad adds an occasional "um hmmm". At first it's hard to tell if this is reserve, shyness or boredom but gradually a streak of bone-dry humor emerges. Asked how winemaking compares to his previous career Brad pauses a beat: "The difference now is, I don't work in an office."

He warms reminiscing about his mentor Russ Raney, the former owner of Evesham Wood. "His wine was only $20 a bottle. It didn't make any economic sense to me to price it that low when it was selling out as soon as we bottled it. So I asked him and he said, 'I want my neighbors to be able to buy it.' That was it. That was his explanation. He loved the people he lived around and knew they couldn't afford more. I liked that a lot."

This burst of enthusiasm says a lot about Brad, the winery, and how it operates. Everything about Illahe from the candle-light racking sessions to its LIVE and Salmon Safe certifications testifies to an unspoken but resoundingly clear ethos: how you do a thing matters. The Fords — Brad, in particular, seem highly attuned to the idea that the process is more important than the outcome. In many businesses this admirable philosophy loses out to profit motives, but not at Illahe.

The Ford family has made a living from the land long enough to understand that making wine in Oregon isn't an ordinary business proposition. It has a high level of inherent, unmitigable risk. Lowell and Bethany swap dates, trying to decide which year the climate dealt the toughest hand. Was it 2013's record-breaking rainfall? The cold summer of 2011? Or sodden 2007, which wine critics wrote off before the vintage was even bottled?

"In 1984 I had to pour water out of my boots when I came in from the vineyard," Lowell recalls, settling the issue.

In 2013 a Pacific typhoon dumped seven inches of rain in two days during harvest. Some producers carried on picking, despite the fact sodden grapes produce dilute wine. Brad, however, got on the phone and literally called the workers in, gambling (successfully, as it happened) on enough subsequent sunshine to dry the crop and allow it to be picked in good condition.

In 2011 they bit their nails through October, hoping the rain would hold off till the grapes ripened. "We were lucky. If we didn't have a long Indian summer we wouldn't have had a harvest." Bethany says this casually, but no harvest is the winemaking equivalent of hitting an iceberg. No fruit means no wine means no sales means a total loss of a year's capital and labor. It's a winery's worst nightmare and in unpredictable Oregon, it could happen.

Dealing with Oregon's climatic vagaries is as much a philosophical as a business decision. Plenty of wineries use technology and chemistry to even out variable fruit, for example, by adding sugar to less-than-perfectly ripe grapes. Brad's genius as a winemaker is in relinquishing the idea that uniformity is a virtue. This contrariness, if you want to call it that, is what makes Illahe wine so good, and so distinctive. As Bethany puts it: "We want to keep the characteristics of the grapes, the vineyard, the winery and not change them. We don't want to just make wine for scores. We want to make wine the way it should be made on the site."

Brad tells me Kafka is one of his favourite writers. "I squished a cockroach this morning. I hope it wasn't Gregor," he jokes. Absurd, implacable misfortunes hit Kafka's characters like tornadoes. The message: you can't control life, but you can choose how to live.

At Illahe this means eschewing the quick fixes of modern technology in favor of experimenting with traditional techniques; embracing and celebrating the exactitude, effort, and attention this entails. One current project is casting pithoi – clay vessels modelled on what the ancient Greeks used to ferment wine – and digging a cave to store them. Brad is lobbying for no electricity, though Bethany wants it wired. Each year on Earth Day Illahe hosts an open-house so people can meet the horses, taste the wine and learn about sustainable growing practices.

The vineyard's output is what Brad drily calls "lower-middle class", about 8000 cases in 2014, because its labor-intensive techniques are antithetical to big production. But then, Kafka didn't write blockbusters. What he did with words, Illahe does with wine: use craft and imagination to create an unforgettable portrait of a place.

For the Salem Trail Guide turn to Page 222.

# Illahe Tasting Notes

### Illahe Pinot Gris 2013
Pale. Crisp apple and pear, lemon notes. Clean mineral finish.

### Illahe Riesling 2012
Straw color. Petrol nose. Mellow mouthfeel. Ripe peach and nectarine with hints of vanilla.

### Illahe Viognier
Slightly acidic nose. Light minerals, peach, pineapple, and fresh citrus. Creamy finish. Perfect picnic wine.

### Illahe Tempranillo Rosé 2013
Pale pink. Light mouthfeel. Strawberry with hints of galia melon. Limited edition of 100 cases sold out in three days.

### Illahe Bon Sauvage Pinot Noir 2012
All-native fermentation, meaning no added yeast. Aged 18 months in oak. Cherry and licorice nose. Silky mouthfeel. Medium tannins and spice. Dark red fruits with a hint of leather.

Coelho Winery
est. 2004

# Coelho

On my first visit to Coelho I miss the turn because the windshield wipers can't move fast enough to make a rift in the solid sheet of April rain. The next time, I recognize the road too late and, once again, must cut through the neighboring gas station to reach the tasting rooms. This is not a mistake the winery's immaculately organized owners would make. Since planting their first vineyards in 2002 the Coelhos have fostered a reputation for order and excellence. They don't make wrong turns.

Coelho means "rabbit" in Portuguese. It is also the family name of Dave and wife Deolinda who took over a decaying hardware store in the blink-and-you'll-miss-it town of Amity to create their vision of a Portuguese wine business. All four of the grown-up Coelho children (plus spouses) are involved in the winery. Sons David and Sam most closely.

Sam strides over to greet me then summons David who reluctantly leaves the lush scarlet climbing rose he's pruning. Tall, blond, blue-eyed Sam has an American Dream glow: part winning-quarterback, part Future Business Leader of America. David is compact and laconic, with dark hair and eyes. He could have stepped out of a 19th century farm scene.

Oregon is young. Even the elders of the Willamette Valley wine industry don't have to look far over their shoulders to see their European heritage. For the Coelhos, however, their Portuguese roots are more than a simple fact of the past. It's the foundation they've chosen to build the winery on. "We're creating a legacy family business," Sam says, seated in the private tasting room at an immense table made of wood reclaimed from an old schoolhouse. "Apparently that takes five generations." He doesn't say according to whom, maybe an old professor. It sounds like the kind of tip you pick up doing a degree in international business and management, which Sam did.

Coelho is where Old World agriculture and winemaking meet New World management and marketing. At first, David and Sam are a too-perfect metaphor: the quiet elder with dirt under his fingernails versus the polished, gregarious younger brother. It is tempting to reduce them – and Coelho Winery – to a simple binary: old versus new, traditional versus modern, farming versus marketing, silver versus gold wedding rings. The longer Sam and David talk, however, the more nuanced the portrait becomes. They have the same distinctive nose, for one thing. For another, they finish each other's sentences, anticipating and riffing like a pair of jazz musicians.

Together, they tell the family story.

The first American Coelhos arrived at Ellis Island in 1914, narrowly escaping the devastation of World War I. They moved to Massachusetts and Rhode Island to start farms and families. A couple of generations later Sam and David's parents were growing 800 acres of tomatoes, sugar beets, corn and alfalfa in the San Joaquin

Valley. Dave Snr. and Deolinda wanted a change from large-scale agriculture. So they headed north with an idea that they could parlay the past into a sustainable future.

Two elements create a successful winery: making and selling. Plenty of winemakers will tell you the latter is more difficult. Especially if you're from Oregon, says Sam, as he reels off figures. Though the fourth-largest wine region in the States (after California, Washington State and New York) Oregon produces a mere 2.5 million cases of wine per year versus California's 350 million. A drop in the proverbial ocean. The challenge is convincing distributors it's worth their while to order a few hundred cases here, a thousand there. Coelho can't sell on volume or scale. It has to make wine that is too good to ignore. So it does.

Dave manages the vineyards but, like everything at Coelho, growing is a family affair. Their agricultural practices date back to the earliest days of winemaking, long before there were such things as chemical herbicides or automated watering systems. They dry farm, meaning no irrigation, and are LIVE certified. These choices place certain demands on both grapes and growers. Vines dig deep to draw water from the soil; workers must be vigilant against pests, fungus, and attuned to the weather. Every year the future hangs on the ancient ritual of harvest.

"In Oregon, you want to get the fruit when it's ready because you never know when it's going to rain," says David. "Sixteen hour days are the shortest I do during harvest."

Sam details a typical day: up before sunrise to

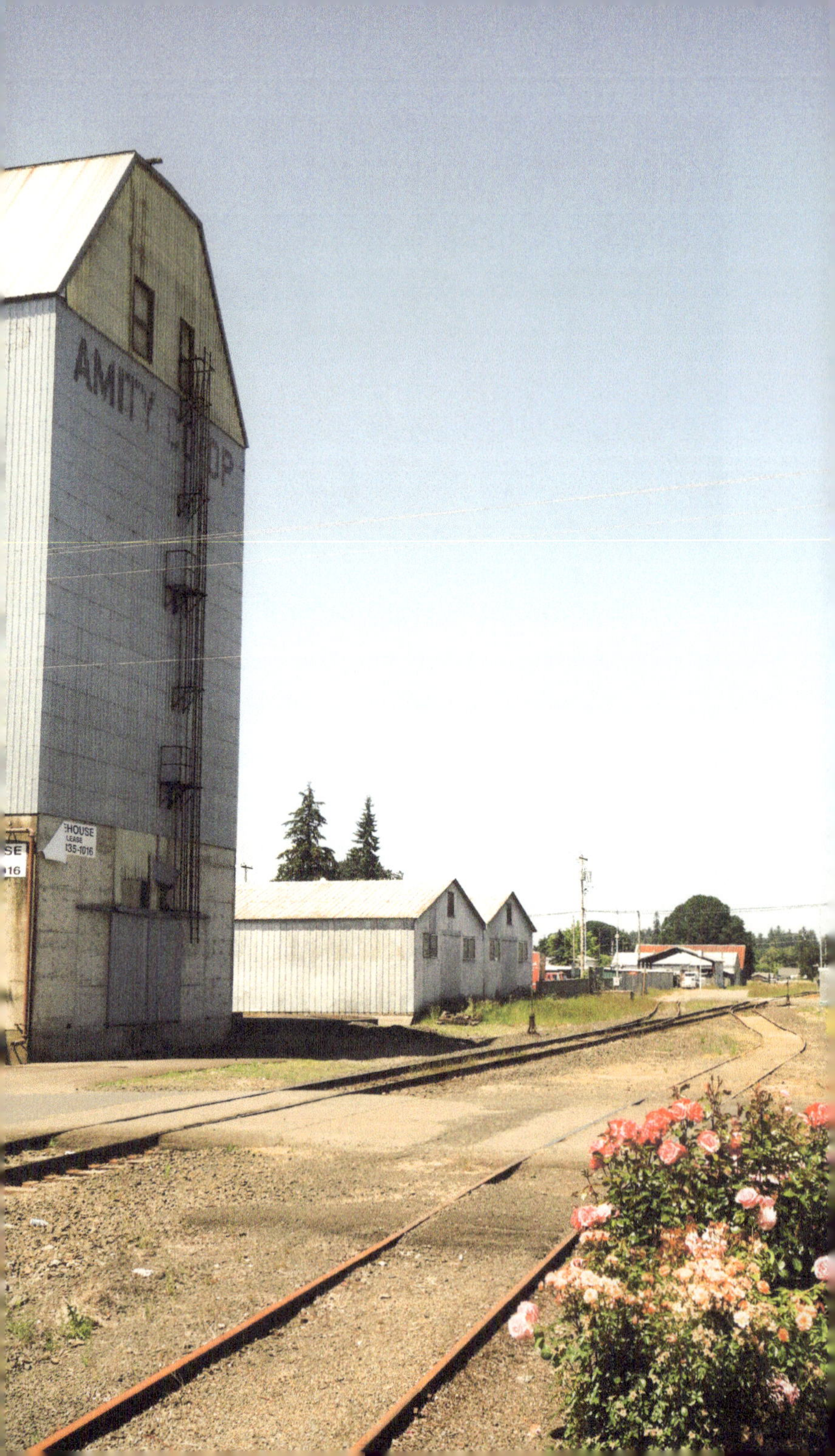
AMITY

load half-ton picking bins on the tractors. "And quarter-ton," David interjects.

His brother effortlessly weaves this interruption into his story, explaining how the growing season determines what size they use. On a dry year they'll have big, healthy clusters of firm grapes that can stand the pressure of being packed a half-ton at a time. If early rains have softened the skins they use smaller bins to protect the fruit. Between 25 and 30 people are in the vineyard during harvest, mostly seasonal workers plus a handful of interns who apply from as far away as France, Serbia, Chile and China. They fill the bins one hand-picked bucket at a time. When the bins are full they are trucked to the winery where David oversees offloading, weighing, hand-sorting and categorization. "You've got your cold-soaking and monitoring, then fermenting for

another two weeks, then –"

"You barrel down," says Sam.

"That's another two weeks," David continues, unperturbed.

"Barrelling down" means the wine goes from steel fermenting tanks, which look like part of a rocket, into French oak. Sam walks me through the barrel room, waving hello to the guy who's hosing them down to slow evaporation. He points out the maker's insignias on the heads. These hand-crafted casks vary by shape ("These are Burgundy, which are squat. A Bordeaux barrel is more elongated") and level of toasting or fire-charring. "Heavy toast" imparts dark chocolate or mocha notes; new oak imparts more overall flavor. Robust wine goes in new barrels; second-use imparts gentler flavors. By the third season a barrel is neutral and used only for storage.

Coelho uses 100% French oak because it is subtler than its American counterpart, yielding silky tannins with delicate fruit and spice. "We make feminine, nuanced, elegant Pinot Noir," Sam says, dropping the "r" in "Noir". "You're going to get earth, spice, fruit, lower alcohol, and vibrant acidity. Our wines age well, they pair well with foods." Old World-style wine, in other words.

Sam leads the way out of the cool storage space into an unseasonably warm spring afternoon. We cross crabgrass to the adjoining warehouse that, in a previous life, stored seed for local farmers. Now it houses Coelho's stock and library wines, cases of every bottling since its 2004 debut. It is precisely 55 degrees Fahrenheit inside. Sam points out his favourite vintages and cases of

Dois Irmãos (Portuguese for "Two Brothers") the brand he and David founded in 2008. The simple white label bears a sketch of them in silhouette, toasting each other with glasses of Pinot.

Back in the tasting room Sam points out an award Coelho Winery won for excellence in a family business. A painting on another wall depicts a great-grandfather on a whaling boat in the Azores – nattily dressed in a dark suit and white shirt. It's a sweet and savvy evocation of the family's work-hard-with-style ethos. The tasting room, with its lofty ceilings, rustic display cabinets, leather sofa and baby grand piano is Old World charm delivered with New World panache. Here they host events like oyster bakes, member's dinners and photo ops with Santa. Local wine buffs stop by to chat and sip robust Tradição – a Portuguese-style wine – or

Serenidade ruby port.

It's all community building, something the Coelhos take literally. David and Sam's mother Deolinda founded the Amity Downtown Improvement Group which was instrumental in bringing lighting, benches, garbage cans and cross-walks to the tiny town.

"It's been wild, the transition," Sam says. And not only for Amity. Coelho Winery's success demonstrates that passion and planning can harness different aptitudes and interests to create a thriving wine business based on Oregon's fine tradition of family collaboration.

For the Salem Trail Guide turn to Page 222.

# Coelho Tasting Notes

**Coelho Paciência Estate Pinot Noir 2012**

Rich color. Spicy, dark fruits, cherry and raisins.

**Coelho Atração Pinot Noir 2012**

Mellow mouthfeel. Bright fruit with a little blackberry and cherry. Vanilla and light spice to finish.

**Dois Irmãos Pinot Noir 2012**

Medium-light body. Plum and black fruit with traces of vanilla. My favorite Coelho Pinot.

**Coelho Tradição Portuguese Red Blend 2012**

Deep ruby color. Medium bodied, smooth. Punchy blackcurrant, black tea, with a hint of dark red licorice.

**Coelho Serenidade Non-Vintage Dessert Wine**

Full body. Robust but smooth. This ruby port-style dessert wine is made from Marechal Foch grapes.

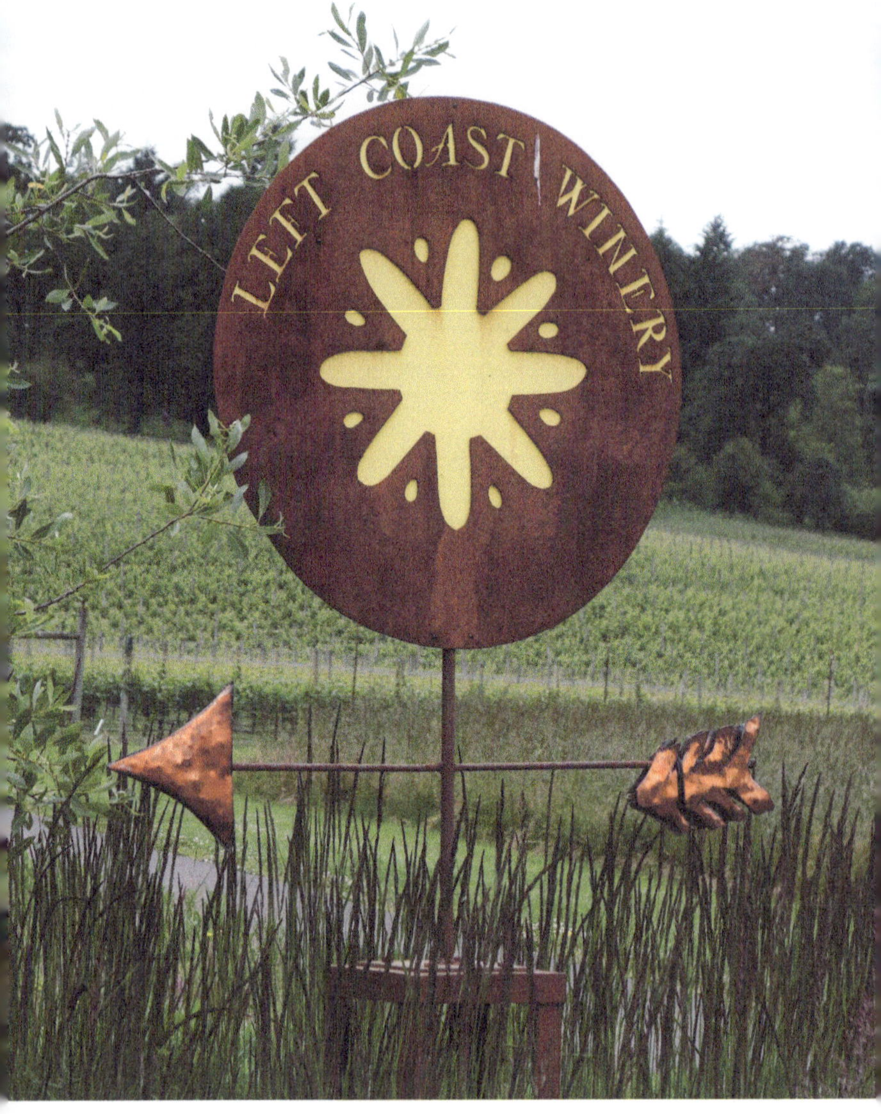
LEFT COAST WINERY

# Left Coast Cellars

When Left Coast Cellars vineyard manager Luke McCollom was six years old he helped his father dig a wine cellar and prune grapes. The die was cast. "I've always been into grapes. Even the generic flavor," he says, voice as unhurried as a sunset. "I liked the grape sodas in the glass bottles, and Bubblicious gum."

Luke got his first job in a winery at age 15. He spent most of his time there polishing its collection of vintage cars but when it got busy he'd help pick grapes, barrel or work the bottling line. The Southern California native went north to San Luis Obispo for college. Before long he swapped environmental engineering for a degree in fruit science, with a minor in wine and viticulture. He also helped found the Central Coast Vineyard Team (now Vineyard Team) – a sustainable agriculture group.

"I've always been into sustainability. Growing up in California I saw how fast freeways and housing tracts developed. I knew the environment was important."

We're sitting in Left Coast Cellar's country-cottage style tasting room and café, surrounded by evidence of Luke's fascination with agriculture and sustainability. Visitors can buy honey produced in the 50-plus beehives that dot the vineyard, jam from its berry patches, fresh-laid eggs, and of course wine. Lupines and purple roses overspill rustic vases. A white-tailed deer waltzes onto the adjoining lawn and stops to graze between two barrel-thick oaks.

Luke is largely responsible for shaping this bucolic scene. When he arrived from California there was just one building on the land and 25 acres of grapes. "Where we're sitting was blackberries and poison oak." He has had a hand in everything for the past 11 years: from the road which he helped tar one Labor Day weekend, to the buildings, vegetable patches, herb gardens, hives and the vineyard which has expanded to 130 acres – 75 of Pinot Noir, 20 of Pinot Gris, 11 of Chardonnay and smaller plantings of Pinot Blanc, Viognier, and Syrah. The total property is 356 acres that includes wetlands, fields and forests.

Everything is symbiotically linked. The luxuriant rose bushes at the ends of the rows are an early warning system for mildew. Grass competes with the vines to encourage fruit production. Rhododendron bushes are honeybee magnets. Solar panels along the edge of the Latitude 45 vineyard power a pump that draws water from the pond, dubbed Lake Suzuki, to feed the drip irrigation system. "The property is a bowl so we gather all our own water. Nobody can pollute it, nothing comes in from outside," Luke says. In addition to absolute purity, this means Left Coast Cellar's combined water and electric bill is about ten bucks a month versus $10,000 or more for a conventionally run property of the same size.

Luke delivers this information with nonchalant pride, like orchestrating an order-of-magnitude energy savings is all in a day's work. For him, it is. Creative viticulture is his calling and he's one of those people who pursue their passion with terrier tenacity. It was his single-minded devotion to Pinot Noir that brought him to Oregon. "I made Pinot in my garage for years. My friends all laughed, but I stuck to it." He cajoled fruit from growers, swapping wine for grapes or hand-picking vines after the main harvest, in order to work with the "rewarding, challenging" grape he loved. When the winemaker job came up at Left Coast Cellars Luke's expertise, enthusiasm and practical engineering skills got him the gig out of a field of 150 applicants.

With a rapidly growing estate to manage, Luke passed head winemaker duties to Joe Wright in 2011. Another Californian with a passion for Pinot, Joe grew up in Burbank, the heart of LA's wonderful world of make-believe. He started to take wine seriously in his early 20s in Aspen, CO, where he supported himself between snowboard seasons by working in a wine shop. "My boss was a huge fan of employee education," Joe says. "He kept pushing me. Ultimately I realized I wanted to make wine."

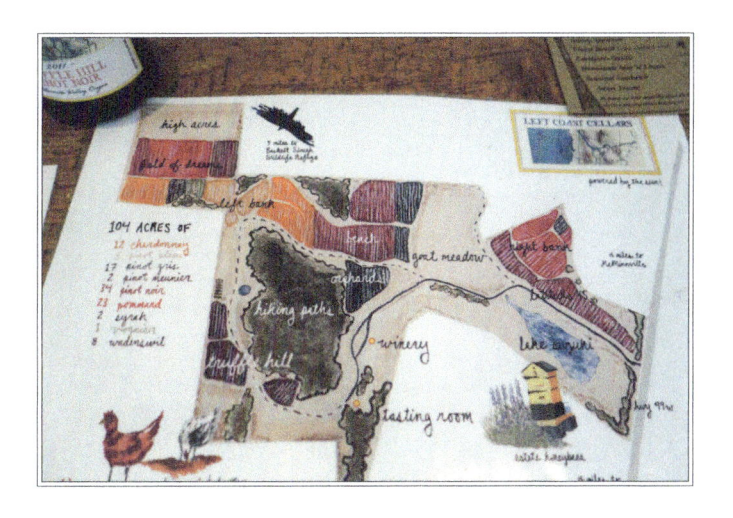

A sales dinner with the Oregon Wine Advisory Board nudged Joe towards the left coast. "I fell in love with Oregon Pinot. Two months later I moved to Oregon with this directory they'd given me. I sat down and called every single winery to ask for a job, starting at A." He got all the way to W, beginning his career at Willamette Valley Vineyards.

Eighteen years on Joe still has a syrupy So-Cal drawl, but he is unswervingly loyal to Oregon and its wine. "I'm here for a reason and it's that," he says, gesturing to the vineyards unspooling in the lee of the winery. "The dirt these vines are growing on." For the record, Left Coast Cellar's dirt is marine sedimentary soil. "When we excavated to build the winery the ground was loaded with seashells. It was a great confirmation of what we taste – this mineral, slate-y foundation for all our wines, red and white."

Everything Joe knows about wine and winemaking he learned on the job and he combines the autodidact's insatiable desire for knowledge with imperturbable patience. "My job used to be, like, 'move these thousand pallets, sweep underneath, then put them back.' Learning to make wine takes a long time. You gotta slow down, allow time to pass, get the experience."

In a more predictable climate experience means figuring out how to do something once, then repeating yourself. Not so in the Willamette Valley. "We essentially have six different vineyards. We're working with different rootstocks, orientations, row composition, even soil composition. There is a lot of opportunity to make different wines. We make five Pinot Noirs and they are truly unique, distinctive from one another.," Joe says. He relishes the challenge: "There hasn't been one vintage like another in the last 18. Things change constantly. You have to shoot from the hip."

Joe's handiwork has garnered numerous 90+ point ratings from Wine Spectator. Asked how that feels he looks into the middle distance and elongates, "Sure" into: "shuuuuurrrrr". Long pause. "Scores are great, I suppose, yeah. But I don't think about them that often, yeah." His mission is to produce wine that is a pure expression of its origin, the rest is none of his business.

Though earnest about winemaking, Joe unwinds

when he hits the topic of the Oregon lifestyle. He vividly describes a Chinese dive bar he discovered in Portland that serves octopus, jellyfish and "freaky, salty cured things" while kitsch horror flicks play in the background. The conversation veers to his outdoor passions. Snowboarding, not so much these days, but he loves mountain bike racing and trail running. "You run? Right on," he enthuses. "You should come with us – the guys from the winery and I go running a couple times a week. We have, like, a 9000-acre back yard just loaded with trails."

Luke shares Joe's appreciation for Oregon life. Both relish the land not just as a source of their livelihood but as a locus for pleasure and social life; a place that defines a way of being. "Oregon, to me, is the final frontier," Luke says, choosing his words with a deliberation his Scottish forebearers would approve. "It was one of the last states where pioneers came. Oregonians are very connected to the land. They care for it. They hold it for generations."

Like all pioneers, Luke has a vision for his territory. He wants to develop separate, simultaneous agriculture programs, managing some vineyards using biodynamics, others following organic protocols, others sustainable. In part, he wants to show people how different ways of growing manifest in the wine. But he has a larger goal, too: "I want to come up with a way of farming that integrates all of these methods and is better than just one."

It is a grand ambition but, based on what he's done to date, entirely feasible. Not just because Luke has a genius for his work, but because he's part of a marvellous natural and human ecosystem. "I believe in a better environment, in people being in tune with their surroundings. In acting like animals, in a way – using our senses in a heightened manner to do the best we can, not just take the easy route."

Unlike humans, animals don't worry about things they can't control. They act with abandon then relax. It's a perfect metaphor for Left Coast Cellars, where hard work is inextricably interwoven with the joy and privilege of nurturing this splendid slice of earth.

For the Salem Trail Guide turn to Page 222.

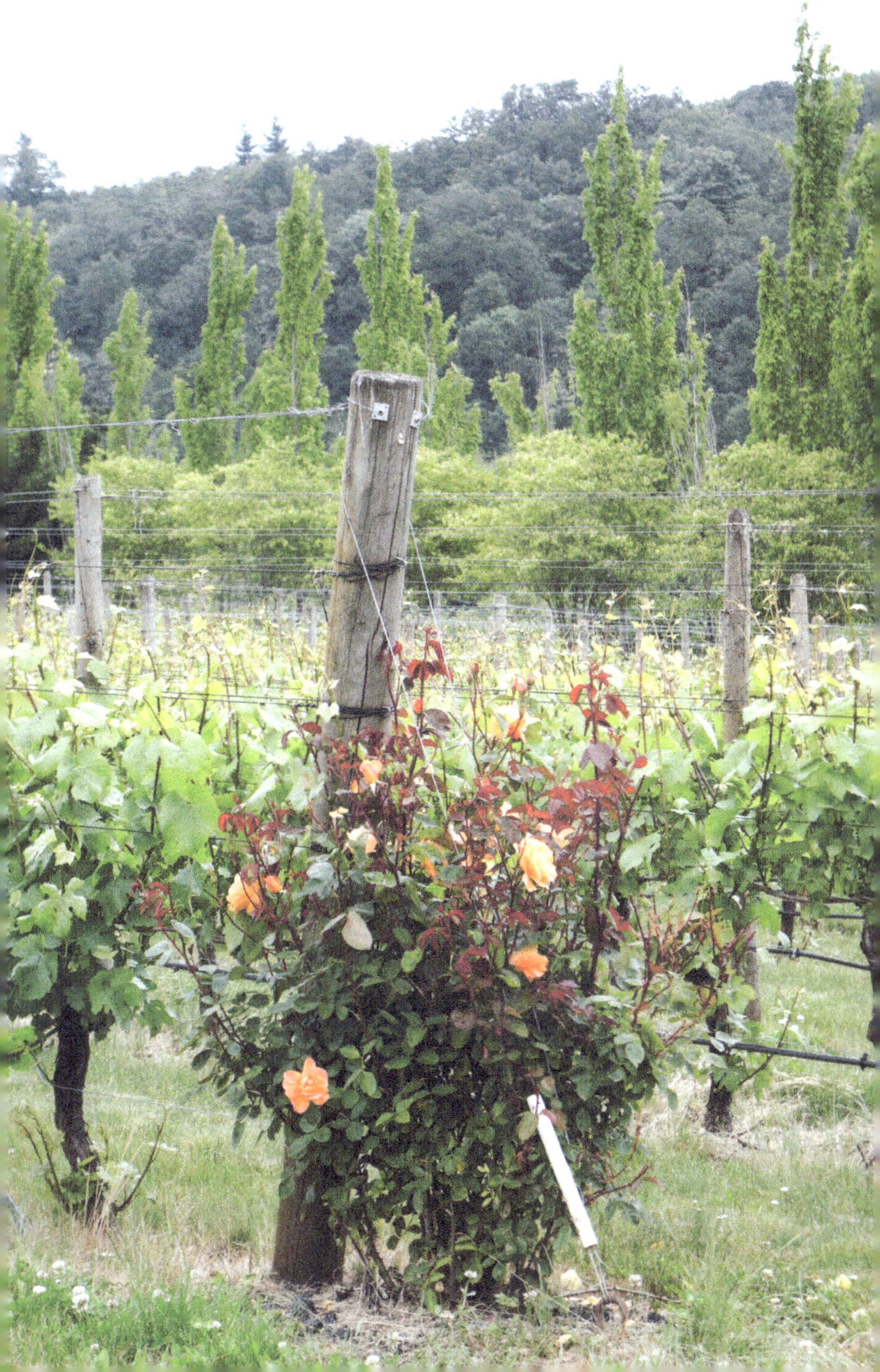

# Left Coast Cellars Tasting Notes

**Left Coast Cellars Viognier Ice Wine 2011**
Sweet honey with ripe peach. White raisin and vanilla notes.

**Left Coast Cellars Orchards Pinot Gris 2013**
Pale straw color. Peach nose. Bright acid. Apple and pear with lemon notes. Clean mineral finish.

**Left Coast Cellars Pinot Noir Rosé 2013**
Medium body. Smooth. Strawberry and ripe red cherry – ideal picnic wine.

**Left Coast Cellars Truffle Hill Chardonnay 2009**
Medium body. Well rounded. Ripe pear and citrus with floral notes.

**Left Coast Cellars Truffle Hill Pinot Noir 2011**
Medium color and body. Punchy petrol nose. Dark fruits, ripe black cherry, robust spice and a hint of leather.

**Left Coast Cellars Latitude 45 Pinot Noir 2011**
Medium color and body but juicier than the Truffle Hill. Ripe fruit with lots of red cherry. Soft spice.

**Left Coast Cellars Right Bank 2011**
Full body. Cherry and red fruit with herbal notes. Like chewing wine gums.

**Left Coast Cellars Suzanne's Pinot Noir 2010**
Full body. Smooth. Rounded black cherry and dark fruits with vanilla. Earthy finish.

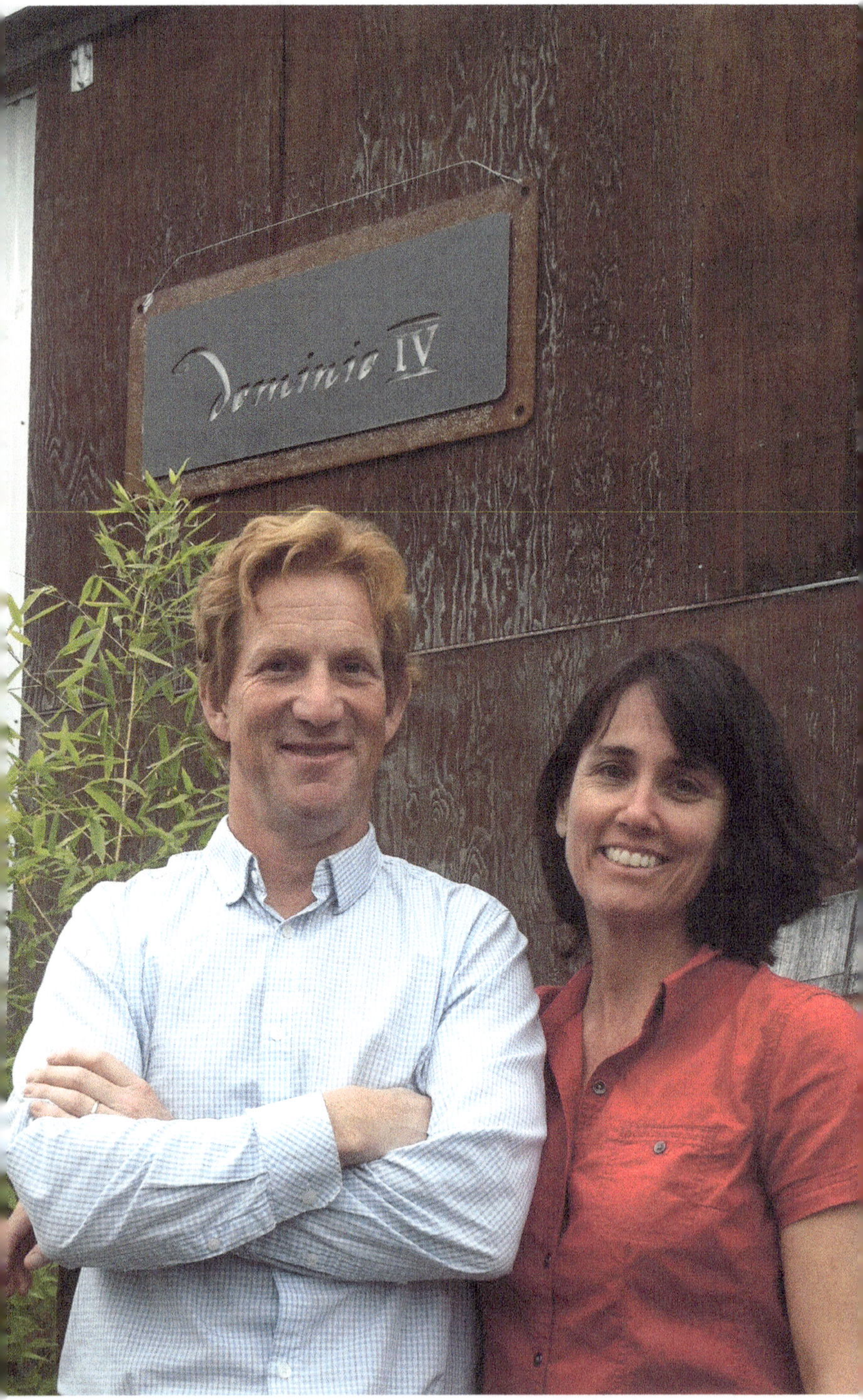
Dominio IV

# Dominio IV

To fully appreciate Dominio IV you have to visit the restroom. While you dry your hands take a good look at the paper-towel holder. Its Art Nouveau-style metalwork is one of the tasting room details hand-crafted by co-owner and winemaker Patrick Reuter. His intellectual energy extends well beyond the confines of enology.

"Patrick wanted to be the great American novelist, but he went into wine," operations and tasting room manager Ryan Kelly-Burnett confides. He points out the Imagination series wines: "He does all the label artwork, names all the wines. He is extremely good at a lot of things."

Ryan, whose role includes working harvest, running the wine club, and compliance, is on the opposite side of a sleek wooden bar. 'OK Computer' plays softly from a docked iPod. Patrick's original artwork dots the walls. The long, narrow room with its high ceiling, dim light and tasteful polished wood fittings evokes a high-grade speakeasy. It is a decadent place to be at 9:30AM.

Patrick arrives, shakes hands then leaves to get coffee. On his return he perches and hooks a scuffed brown brogue onto the rung of his bar-stool. With his navy sport coat and cuffed dark denim jeans he could pass for a hip college professor or successful novelist. But when he speaks there is no mistaking him for anything but a winemaker. Before the coffee even kicks in he's explaining the origins of biodynamic farming, which he wryly defines as "slightly eccentric people doing intensive agriculture", and describing how he and wife Leigh Bartholomew founded Dominio IV.

The story starts back at University of Oregon where the couple met, though it was only after they graduated and got office jobs that they considered the wine business. "We'd always enjoyed wine together and it dawned on us that the people who made wine were paid to make wine. We could make a living off it. That sounded exciting."

Leigh and Patrick headed south to UC Davis's legendary wine program They picked complementary courses: she studied viticulture – grape-growing – and Patrick focused on terroir, learning how to make the best wine possible from a given place. After graduation they hit the road to hone their craft, working at wineries in New Zealand, Chile, France, Washington State and California. Ultimately, Oregon called them back. "Here, you're in a verdant, healthy, alive place," Patrick says. "There is an abundance, especially of water. From a people standpoint, it's a real community of helpfulness and cooperation."

Community and cooperation are two words every winemaker I meet mentions and for small outfits like Dominio the collaborative, open spirit of Oregon is vital to survival and success. For the first few years Dominio made wine in a cooperative facility using rented gear. Now it co-owns equipment and shares workspace with Lumos winery. "To start off you have to be extremely wealthy or a lot naïve," Patrick says, laughing. "We were broke. All we had were grapes and barrels." Fortunately, they have exceptional grapes.

Three Sleeps, Dominio IV's estate vineyard, is in the Columbia River Gorge just outside Mosier, OR. "It used to be an organic cherry orchard, virgin land, so we said, let's do this biodynamically." It is 15 acres of wilderness, eight of which are planted in grapes. The rest is home to an abundance of plants including dozens of fruit trees, plus birds, sheep, horses and migrant wild creatures. Patrick also wants a cow. "That's the apex of biodynamics," he says wistfully. "To have a bovine on the property."

Even without a resident bovine the vineyard produces top-class Tempranillo, Syrah and Viognier. All three are warm weather grapes more commonly grown in California. For Patrick and co that just adds to the fun. "Oregon can do more than Pinot Noir and Chardonnay," he says. "Climates like the Columbia Gorge and southern Oregon can do amazing things with these varieties. We wanted to explore that."

This experimental ethos contributes to the winery's chummy, collegial atmosphere. The staff of five all pitch in to do what needs to be done, including tasting the wine as they blend. "Everybody's influence matters, which is awesome," Ryan enthuses. "The diversity of our palates shows in the finished product." He's lined up eight bottles and an equal number of voluminous glasses and is eyeing our progress on the coffee. Usually the tasting room is only open Friday and Saturday so this is a bonus opportunity for him to show off his beloved vintages.

Ryan's zest for wine in general and Dominio IV in particular is characteristic of a new breed of pioneers who embrace a definably Oregonian way of life and making a living. There is one in practically every vineyard or winery, hailing from places like Texas, Missouri, New Jersey and – in Ryan's case – Georgia. "Here, you start a conversation by asking, 'Where are you from?'" he notes. "All my mates are transplants. Nobody is a native but we're Oregonians now, by choice."

What makes Oregon so special?

"The diversity and overall energy. We have a simpler mindset but are progressive at the same time. There's a sense of holding on to the integrity of things while still bringing in new ideas."

Normally this bright-eyed spiel would have me reaching for the spit bucket but Ryan is on the level. His delight is infectious, especially when we start tasting wine. Mindful of the early hour and the drive home I take dainty sips and awkward spits. He tosses back great mouthfuls then expels rich purple streams into the bucket. "Don't worry," he says. "Sometimes you have to pour it away."

Winemaking à la Dominio IV is a lot about letting go, about accepting what the land and climate yield and not getting stuck on fixed ideas. "Seventy to eighty percent of what you taste is vineyard," Ryan says. "Our job as winemakers is to help out on the bad years and not screw it up on the good years."

Viognier and Pinot are temperamental to grow; Tempranillo gets tricky once it comes off the vine. "Pinot is a heartbreak grape but Tempranillo is a harder wine to make," notes Patrick. "You have to trust your intuition and not fight it." We taste the 2009 Midnight Skies Tempranillo (other bottlings: "Rain on Leaves", "Valley of the Angels", "Penny for a Lily") – it is as robust as a brawl in a bodega, with spicy clove and pepper notes and rich black cherry fruit. I decide it won't hurt to drink just this one.

Dominio IV's pervasive elegance, originality and beauty wouldn't be possible without Leigh's tireless work as a viticulturist, nurturing the Dominio IV vineyards and providing a steady income through the years. She worked at Archery Summit for 14 years and now manages Domaine Drouhin's properties. Leigh and Patrick also have two sons. "She does a lot," her husband says. "It's impressive." The family affair extends to her parents, who co-own Three Sleeps vineyard and run a small bed-and-breakfast there. "From the front porch," he jokes. "Martini in hand."

What's the secret to success as a working couple?

"That's easy. We leave each other's domains alone."

We move on to taste the Imagination series (the ones with Patrick's gorgeous artwork on the labels).

Dominio IV
Imagination Series no. 2
Quail Run
2011

These are tiny production runs of wines from specific sites. Specific as in, rows of a vineyard. "You can walk the land this comes from in a few minutes and see every vine," Patrick says. "We want people to know what a piece of earth tastes like. It's an articulation of place." With several bottles to go he excuses himself to get back to work, leaving Ryan and I to the wine.

"How did you end up at Dominio?" I ask. Ryan pours Imagination No. 3, a soft rosé made by adding whole clusters of Syrah to Viognier. "I met Patrick and grabbed a few bottles of his Viognier without trying it. When I got back to Georgia and drank it I was like, shit, I gotta make this." So he headed back to Oregon. Patrick and Leigh, recognizing a fellow adventurer, invited him to join the team.

"Dominio is addictive," he grins. "I get to work with such intelligent, creative people."

Later, when we've conquered the bottle row, he shows me around the warehouse. Mordechai, a surf-loving California native with an immense, wiry beard, is labelling a case of Imagination No. 3. He uses a cardboard bottle rest to align each label before smoothing it gently from the centre to the edges, pressing out any air-bubbles before he polishes the bottles on the hem of his black tee-shirt. He and Ryan slip into industry gossip. Californian mega-brand Kendall-Jackson recently purchased property nearby. They speculate it will drive up the price of grapes but Ryan is upbeat: "If it gets 'Willamette Valley' on labels around the world, it can only be good for us."

He's right on two levels. Business-wise, Dominio IV has little to do with the Kendall-Jackson's of the wine world. Their economies are unrelated; their practices and product are distinct; they don't compete for an audience. More importantly, it inhabits a different psychic space. Dominio means 'domain'. By building on creativity, collaboration, loyalty, hard work and imagination it has staked out a territory that no one can dispute.

For the McMinnville Trail Guide turn to Page 218.

# Dominio IV Tasting Notes

**Dominio IV Imagination No. 1 Grenache-Syrah**
Deep color. Medium body. Red cherry fruit with a hint of cedar wood.

**Dominio IV Imagination No. 2 Riesling**
Medium body. Pineapple and green apple. Not too sweet.

**Dominio IV Imagination No. 3 Viognier-Syrah**
Soft pink color. Mellow mouthfeel. Strawberry and red fruits. Made by dropping whole Syrah grapes into Viognier.

**Dominio IV Tapis Pinot Noir 2009**
Light body. Red berries, red cherry, licorice, hint of tobacco. Light tannins.

**Dominio IV Rain on Leaves Pinot Noir 2010**
Mellow mouthfeel. Smooth, rounded deep cherry with vanilla essence.

**Dominio IV Valley of the Angels Syrah 2008**
Deep color. Rich, full body. Black cherry and blackcurrant, peppery. Irresistible.

**Dominio IV Midnight Skies Tempranillo 2009**
Robust. Rich, complex, black cherry, clove and spice.

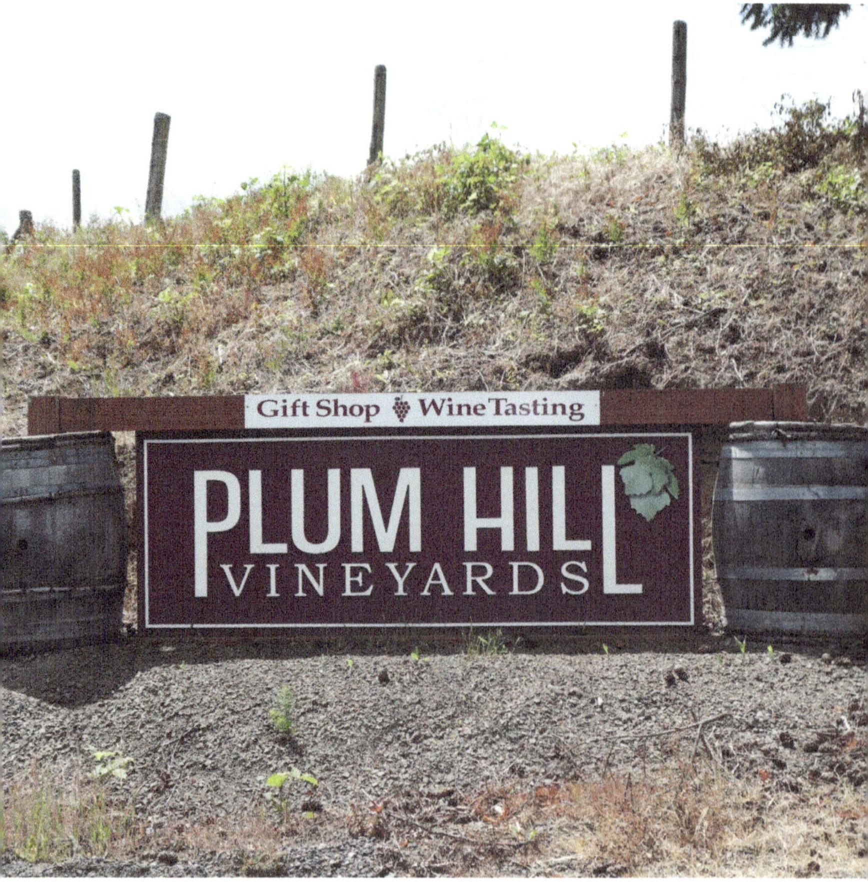
Gift Shop Wine Tasting
PLUM HILL
VINEYARDS

# Plum Hill

Fifty-four inches. That's the perfect height for a tasting room bar according to RJ Lint. He knows because he and wife Juanita took a tape-measure when they went wine-tasting and sized up every bar in every vineyard they visited.

Since buying Plum Hill's main property in 2007 Juanita and RJ have devoted themselves to creating a winery where "welcome" isn't just a word on the doormat. "Our philosophy is to treat customers the way we want to be treated," RJ explains, beaming from beneath a faded black Plum Hill baseball cap. "Wine is social. We want the customer to have an exceptional experience and feel comfortable here."

It was my brother and sister-in-law who introduced me to Plum Hill wine. We opened a bottle for dinner one night and it went indecently quick. So, one sunny afternoon, we drove the few miles through rolling farm country from Forest Grove, past the L Bar T bison ranch, to the Plum Hill vineyard and tasting room near Gaston. When I return to interview the Lints, more than a year later, I mention this to Juanita.

"Oh yes!" she beams. "I know your sister-in-law, she brought some people in the other day."

Plum Hill is like a real-life *Cheers*. They remember names, birthdays and wine preferences. There's a dog-run outside for folk's four-footed pals and barstools so visitors will take it easy and stay a while. They host live music on the broad patio overlooking the vineyard and encourage guests to picnic beneath the giant oaks. Juanita wants to turn the house on the property into a B&B and expand the facilities so they can host weddings. "We like people," RJ grins. "We want to get to know you, we want you to relax, we want you to have a good time and enjoy the wine."

This ambition is all the more generous for the fact that RJ and Juanita didn't need to do any of this. In fact, they would have been better off, financially anyway, choosing a conventional retirement. Both were telecommunications professionals working for companies like Bell Labs, AT&T, and Integra. They were dedicated and successful. Juanita travelled a lot. RJ was a consultant for the Australian government at one point. They'd earned leisure time and then some.

But Juanita had a job that brought them to the Willamette Valley and RJ, recently retired, was curious about winemaking. He started volunteering at vineyards then bought a two-acre plot in Forest Grove. When Juanita reached retirement she stayed active running craft bazaars and women's groups. They both volunteered at their church. "We never really stopped," she admits. "It's fitting for us to put our energy into something like this."

She modestly elides the fact that planting a vineyard and building a winery is a whole different scale of difficult than organizing church groups. Neither had any professional training in the wine industry, nor background in marketing or customer service. But they had a dream.

RJ went to UC Davis to study small-vineyard management, returning to continue his education at Chemeketa's Wine Studies Center. Juanita dove into the arcane and sometimes maddening world of administration, marketing, sourcing, networking, and compliance.

"Did you know," she asks, "that every single wine label design has to be approved by the federal government? Sometimes you send three identical labels and only two get approved. Who knows why?"

Also: Did you know that when you plant a new varietal you're not allowed to bottle it until you've sent the government documentation of its characteristics and qualities?

And: Did you know there are 32 pages of federal

requirements to fulfil in order to get an AVA [American Viticultural Area] designation?

I didn't know. Nor do most people who park beside the dog-run and pass the wine-bottle water fountain on the way into Plum Hill's cozy tasting room. That's okay though because, despite the mountains of paperwork and snares of bureaucracy, the Lints love with what they do. "RJ's day doesn't start till he gets to the vineyard," Juanita tells me as I sip a glass of vanilla-scented oaked Pinot Gris. "I get my social fix right here."

She has transformed the space into a veritable garden of wine-lovers' delights with an atmosphere that is half-chic and half country kitchen. An old-fashioned red and gold popcorn cart stands in the middle of the room. Shelves are neatly but abundantly filled with local produce like hazelnuts and wine salt; gourmet snacks;

quirky gifts; drinking accessories (the $29 cork cages "sell like crazy"); hand-drawn greeting cards by local artists; napkins and table-runners. Juanita sews these herself. It's a break from thinking about selling wine, she says, but the fruits of her work still end up in the tasting room.

    Not that she'd want it any other way. After so many years of business travel and the corporate realm Juanita relishes the world coming to her and the conviviality of small town life. "The community is fabulous," she says. Most weekends Juanita can be found running a booth at the Forest Grove farmer's market, or showcasing Plum Hill wines at local events like Forest Grove UnCorked, or winemaker's dinners. She and RJ open the tasting room doors for charity, too. Canines Uncorked, an Oregon Humane Society fundraiser, saw Plum Hill overrun with a pack of 80 pets enjoying everything from doggy psychics to pooch sundaes while their humans sipped wine.

There is no mistaking Juanita and RJ's zest for what they do. Or how hard they work to transform aspirations into reality. When they bought the property there was no vineyard, only the buildings from its previous incarnation as a dairy farm. RJ reckoned it was promising land, set as it is between Montinore and Patton Valley wineries. He called in opinions from friends at various vineyards, including Kramer and Purple Cow. Looks good, was the consensus. So Juanita and RJ politely ignored their financial adviser's views on the matter and bought it.

"What advice would you give someone who wanted to get into the wine business?" I ask.

"I'd probably tell them not to," Juanita says. "Unless you have a backer who's okay with not making money. We thought we had enough capital to get us up and running but it wasn't even a drop in the bucket."

"It wasn't close to enough," her husband shrugs.

But they're both smiling.

Outside, the vineyard unfurls down the hillside, overlooked by a wind-snapped American flag. They have 33 acres planted here, plus two in their Forest Grove plot, and another 18 a friend farms for them. This supplies enough fruit to make between 900-1600 cases a year – a variation due to Oregon's climatic uncertainties.

Their philosophy of making Plum Hill as comfortable as possible for visitors extends to its vines. After much study and thought RJ came to question the "common knowledge" that stressed plants produce better fruit. "I created my own theory, the 'happy plant theory', which is that if the plants are happy the fruit will be good. That's my strategy. If it needs fertiliser it will get it, if it doesn't, it won't; if it needs water, it'll get water." His John Goodman-esque delivery makes everything sound half in jest, but RJ is dead serious about his vineyard. His labor-intensive practices, including high-density planting, thinning shoots by hand, and avoiding harsh herbicides and pesticides, ensure top quality fruit. And they name the plants, in case there's any truth to the notion that talking to them helps them grow. Visitors can stroll along the rows and get acquainted with The Grape Gatsby, Albert Vinestein, Oprah Winefry, Babe Root, and Mama Cask, among others.

    Proof of any viticultural theory is in the bottle and Plum Hill wines sing resounding praise of the happy plant ethos. Distinctive, and often experimental, the vineyard boasts a surprising number of varietals for its size including Pinot Noir, Pinot Gris, Pinot Blanc, Riesling, Schönburger (Oregon's only commercial planting of this rare Muscat/Pinot Noir cross) and Syrah. The latter is a newcomer. Another experiment. "It isn't supposed to get ripe at this end of the valley," RJ says, looking not in the least concerned. He reckons he can make a 12% Syrah from his cool climate grapes versus the 14-15% typical of California Syrah. "I thought, let's plant some, even though all the academics say it won't get ripe. Sometimes you gotta just try it on your own."

Just try, might as well be Plum Hill's motto. By combining venturesome winemaking and indefatigable hospitality Juanita and RJ exemplify the spirit of Willamette Valley wine country. And make every visit to Plum Hill feel like a homecoming.

For the Forest Grove Trail Guide turn to Page 206.

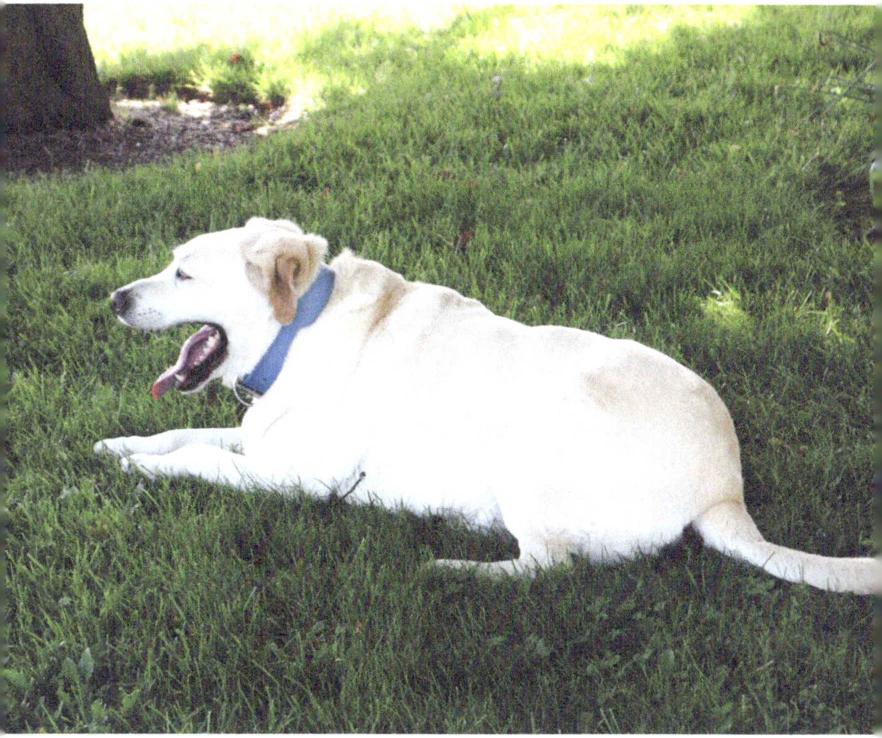

# Plum Hill Tasting Notes

**Plum Hill Chardonnay 2012**

Hint of pink from ageing in Syrah barrels. Fresh green apple and pear, citrus notes.

**Plum Hill Pinot Gris 2011**

Medium body. Intense aromatic vanilla nose and flavor from ageing in uncharred oak. Lemon notes. Light acid.

**Plum Hill Riesling 2012**

Very pale. Citrus and gentle sweetness. A relaxed, easy-to-drink wine.

**Plum Hill Barrel Select Pinot Noir 2011**

Medium body. Wine gum nose. Light, silky mouthfeel. Redcurrant and raspberry fruit with hint of vanilla.

**Plum Hill Winemakers Barrel Select 2011**

Medium color. Tastes darker than it looks. Plummy with blackberry and fresh red cherry fruit.

**Plum Hill Syrah 2011**

Dark color. Spicy nose. Rounded blackberry jam and ripe currant, hint of cedar wood. Damn near edible.

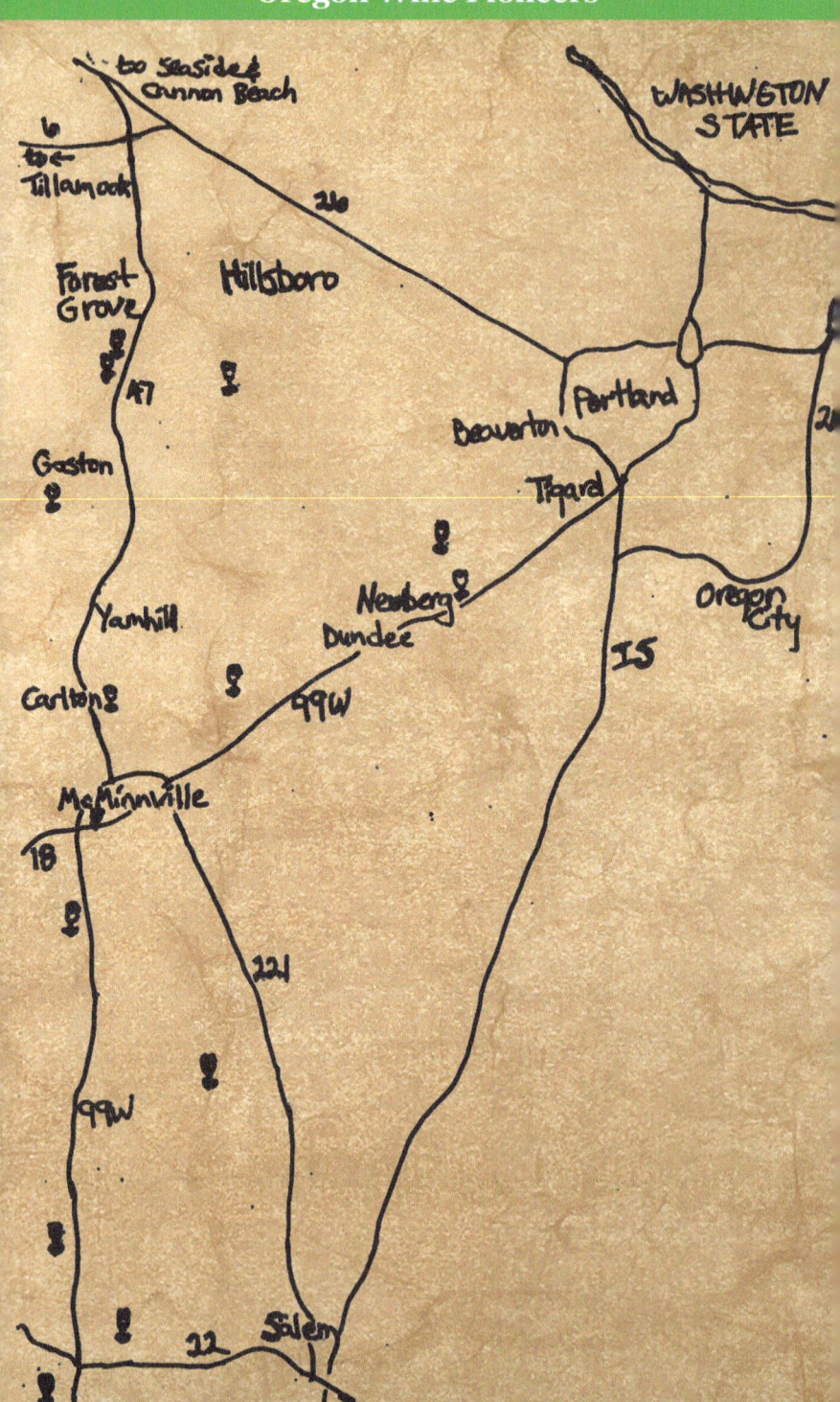

# Oregon Wine Pioneers

# Welcome to Oregon

This guide is meant to serve as the starting point for your Oregon Wine Journey. Along with directions and contact details for each of the wineries featured in the book you will find information and descriptions of select local restaurants recommended by the owners and employees of the wineries we visited.

When touring Oregon always travel by the oldest, narrowest, and most winding road you can find. Slow down. Soak up the natural beauty. Study the agricultural diversity and abundance. Stop at the small farms advertising diverse goods via handmade signs.

If you are starting from Oregon's most populous city, Portland, turn to the next page.

If you are starting from Oregon's Capitol, Salem, turn to page 222.

If you are coming up from Southern Oregon or California via Interstate 5 turn to page 228.

If you are starting in McMinnville turn to page 218.

If you are starting in Newberg turn to page 212.

If you are starting in Forest Grove turn to page 206.

# Oregon Wine Pioneers

# Portland

"There's no pity in the rose city" is a favorite chant of fans of the Timbers, Portland's professional soccer (football) team, but in truth the City of Roses is renowned for the kindness of its inhabitants, as well as their fondness for beer, which flows freely at the dozens of craft brewing establishments that dot the city.

The list of places to go and things to see and do in Portland is too long to relate here, but you should have no difficulty in finding something to suit your tastes. Free weeklies like *Portland Mercury* and *Willamette Week* are good sources of information and event listings.

One restaurant that should not be missed when visiting Portland is *Seasons and Regions*, a refreshingly unpretentious eatery that serves fresh Oregon seafood along with dishes built around locally grown produce.

Beer lovers will want to stop at the *Widmer Gasthaus Pub* or *Deschutes Brewery Portland Public House* to sample a wide variety of specialty brews that never make it onto store shelves.

Once you are ready to hit the road the two best routes out of Portland are to go South to Newberg via *Ponzi Vineyards*, or to head West to Forest Grove.

**Ponzi Vineyards**
(503) 628-1227
19500 SW Mountain Home Rd, Sherwood, OR 97140

# Portland Trail Guide

Head West on Sunset Highway/Hwy 26 and take exit 69A for Oregon 217 South and follow to exit 4B for Scholl's Ferry Road/210. Take a right onto highway 210. Follow 210 for about 9 miles then continue onto 219. Turn left on SW Mountain Home Road. Page 60.

Continue past *Ponzi Vineyards* on Highway 219 for a spectacular scenic drive to Newberg. Page 212.

**Forest Grove**
Head West on Sunset Highway/Hwy 26 over Portland's West Hills, past Washington Park and the Oregon Zoo. Take Exit 57 and turn left onto Glencoe Rd. After 1.3 miles turn right onto NW Zion Church Rd. After 2 miles continue onto NW Cornelius Schefflin Rd. In 1.6 miles at the roundabout take the first exit onto NW Verboort Rd. After 0.4 miles take the third exit from the roundabout onto NW Martin Rd. After 2 miles turn left onto Quince St, then turn right on Pacific Ave, which goes into Forest Grove. Page 206.

**Newberg & McMinnville**
Head South from the city center on Interstate 5 and take exit 289 toward Tualatin/Sherwood. Follow Tualatin Sherwood Road for 4.6 miles then turn left on 99 West, which leads to Newberg. Page 212.

**Salem & Southern Oregon**
Follow Interstate 5 South to Salem. Page 224.

# Oregon Wine Pioneers

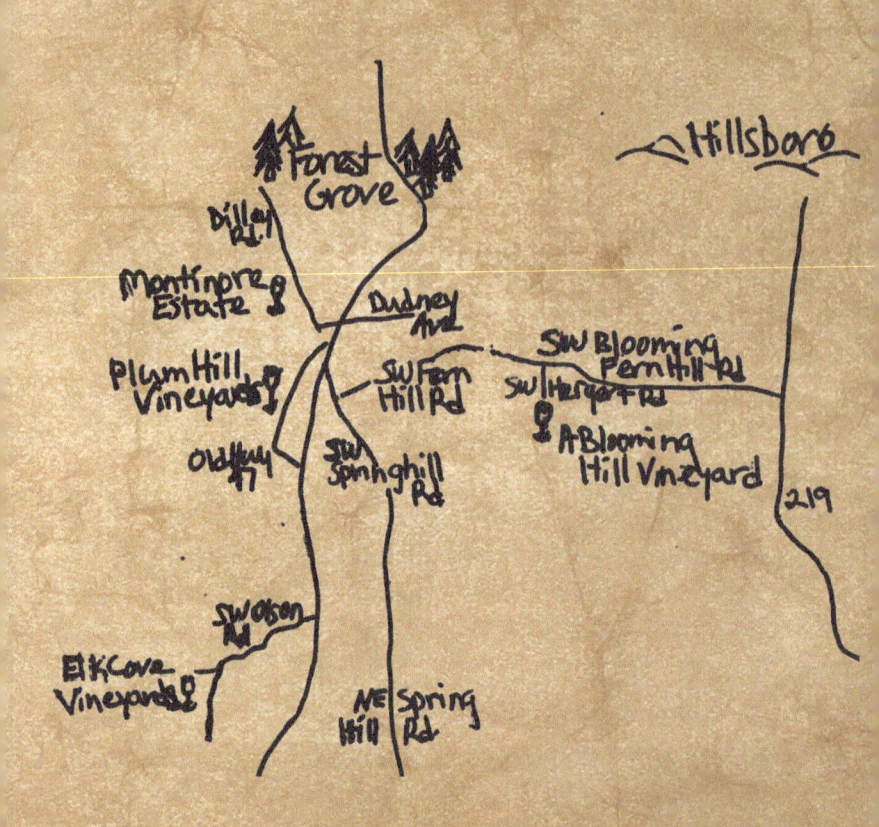

# Forest Grove Trail Guide

# Forest Grove

Forest Grove is home to Pacific University and the heart of the Sip47 Wine Route. You will find *A Blooming Hill Vineyard*, *Elk Cove*, *Montinore*, *Plum Hill* and a number of restaurants nearby.

From Forest Grove continue South on Highway 47 all the way to McMinnville. Page 218. Alternately, take Highway 240 at Yamhill to cut over to Newberg. Page 212.

### A Blooming Hill Vineyard
(503) 359-4706
5195 SW Hergert Rd, Cornelius, OR 97113

From Highway 8 head South on Highway 47 and take a left on SW Fern Hill Road. After 1.5 miles take a left onto SW Blooming Fern Hill Road and then take a right onto SW Hergert Road after one mile. Page 122.

### Elk Cove
(503) 985-7760
27751 NW Olson Rd, Gaston, OR 97119

Follow Tualatin Valley Highway/47 to Gaston and take a right on NW Olson Road at the Post Office. *Elk Cove* will be about 3 miles up on your right. Page 34.

### Montinore
(503) 359-5012
3663 SW Dilley Rd, Forest Grove, OR 97116

# Oregon Wine Pioneers

Take OR 47 South. Take a right on Dudney Road and another right on Dilley Road. Page 72.

**Plum Hill**
(503) 359-4706
6505 Southwest Old Highway 47, Gaston, OR 97119

From Forest Grove head South on Oregon 47. Take a slight right onto Old Highway 47, proceed 1.1 miles and *Plum Hill* will be on your right. Page 188.

## Restaurants

**One Horse Tavern**
(503) 985-3273
300 Front St, Gaston, OR 97119

*They say:* An independently-owned bar and grill nestled among wineries and the scenic Highway 47 to the coast. We believe that a restaurant and bar is more than just a place to get a bite to eat. It's a place to form friendships and community connections, a home away from home, and at The One Horse, a place where first timers are made to feel as welcome as our most loyal regulars.

*We say:* Quirky local dive with class. Holly Witte of *A Blooming Hill Vineyards* praises its food, music and especially the artful glass mosaics created by owner Wendy Chamberlain.

*Don't miss:* Weiner Wednesdays. Options include the Wolf Man Jack, made with grilled onions, cheese, bacon cooked with Jack Daniels – plus an optional shot of JD.

**1910 Main**
(503) 430-7014
1910 Main St., Suite A, Forest Grove, OR 97116

*They say:* Located in historic downtown Forest Grove. 1910 Main offers classic American food that is comfort food at its finest. The cuisine will take diners back to a nostalgic era in American cooking, bringing updated twists by using local food and beverages.

*We say:* Top pick from Juanita and RJ at *Plum Hill Vineyards*, 1910 offers a homey atmosphere and grown-up versions of childhood favourites like burgers, mac 'n' cheese, meatloaf and door-stop sandwiches. All accompanied by wine from its award-winning cellar.

*Don't miss:* Save space for the marionberry crisp served with Tillamook vanilla ice cream. Fridays and Saturdays feast on prime rib with mashed Yukon potatoes.

**Primrose & Tumbleweeds**
(503) 703-8525
248 E Main St, Hillsboro, OR 97123

*They say:* We are excited to offer The World's Largest Selection of Oregon Wines, over 200 hand-crafted beers, and the largest selection of hard cider on the west side of Portland. We offer 10 rotating taps with local beers and hard ciders. Our "Today's Pour" list rotates frequently so each time you come in you will be able to taste a different

Oregon Wine. Wine can also be purchased off the shelf and enjoyed with appetizers, soups, sandwiches or a decadent dessert.

*We say:* One wine bar you don't want to miss and won't want to leave. With over 4000 wines you are more than spoiled for choice. We love that you can buy a bottle and they'll open it for you to enjoy with your meal, no corkage fee. That's plain cool.

*Don't miss:* Happy hour from 3-6PM Monday to Friday, and whisky flights in the Tumbleweed Saloon every Friday and Saturday from 6PM to close.

**Syun Izakaya**
(503) 640-3131
209 NE Lincoln St, Hillsboro, OR 97124

*They say:* A family-owned, award-winning place for Japanese pub-style dishes, top-notch sushi and sashimi, and superb sake. SYUN is an authentic Japanese restaurant featuring many types of hot and cold small dishes, a large variety of amazing sushi creations, noodle dishes, salads and unique deserts. We also boast the most impressive sake collection in the area.

*We say:* The "best Japanese restaurant either of us have been to anywhere" according to Jim and Holly Witte – high praise indeed coming from a couple who've lived in New York City, Los Angeles, Seattle and Portland. It's also been named one of the Top 15 Japanese Restaurants in the US by Zagat. We like its commitment to using local, organic produce and sourcing sustainable fish.

*Don't miss:* Sashimi for the seafood purists – including smoked salmon, toro and amberjack. For cooked food try the Donburi rice bowls and home-made dumplings.

## Urban Decanter
(503) 359-7678
2030 Main St, Forest Grove, OR 97116

*They say:* A wine bar, wine and beer shop and restaurant in the beautiful Willamette Valley. We have wines by the glass, bottles for sale, live music every Saturday night, and wine flights every Friday night. The menu incorporates local, fresh produce from the Willamette Valley, highlighting our commitment to sustainable, community-sourced food. Our food, wine, and craft beer specials change frequently, so come see what we are all about!

*We say:* Owned by Rebecca Kramer (of the *Kramer Vineyards* family) this is a wine shop for enthusiasts that doubles as a neighborhood hangout. You can easily pop in to pick up a bottle for dinner and find yourself there hours later, with a handful of new best friends.

*Don't miss:* Friday night wine tastings featuring a rotation of local vineyards. Start Saturday with the ultimate hair of the dog: five-buck mimosas then stick around for live music.

# Oregon Wine Pioneers

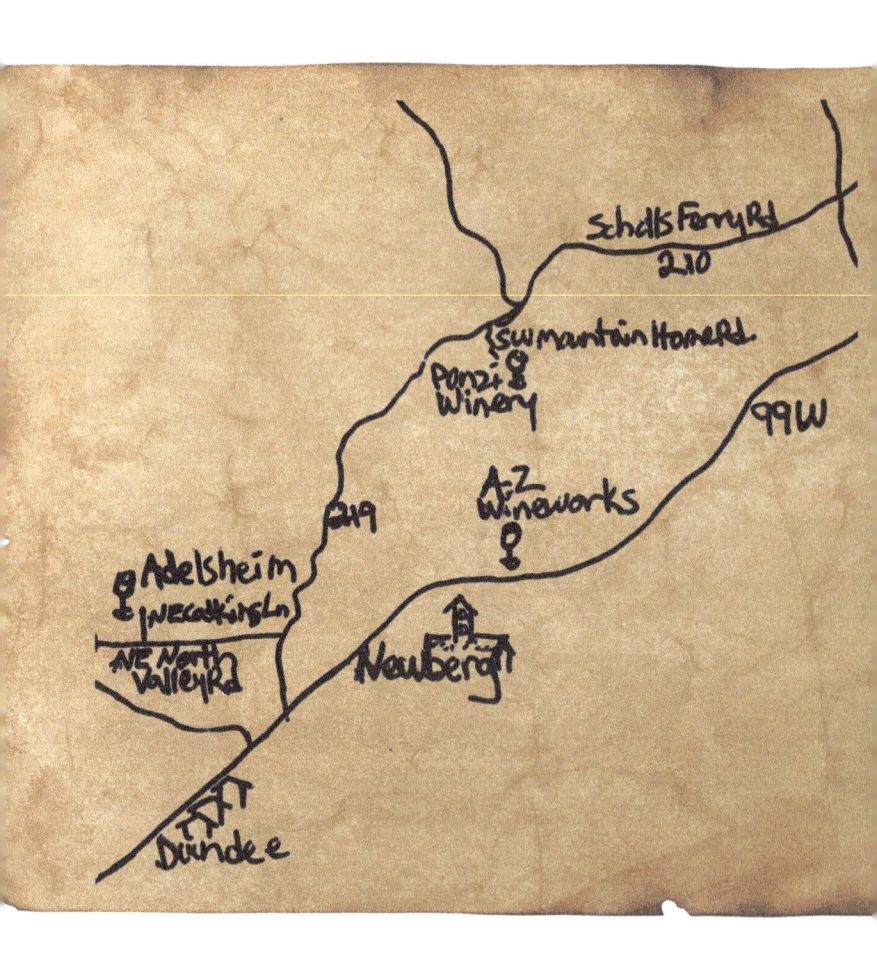

**Newberg Trail Guide**

# Newberg

Newberg, Dundee and their surrounding hillsides are home to dozens of wineries, vineyards, including *Adelsheim*, and *A to Z Wineworks*.

### Adelsheim
(503) 538-3652
16800 NE Calkins Ln, Newberg, OR 97132

From 99W Southbound take a right onto Highway 240 / Main St. Take a right onto NE Stone Road, then take a left onto NE North Valley Road and take a right onto NE Calkins Lane. Page 22.

### A to Z Wineworks
(503) 554-1918
30835 OR-99W, Newberg, OR 97132

*A to Z* is on 99W about 3 miles North of the center of Newberg. Page 46.

## Restaurants

### JORY
(503) 554-2526
2525 Allison Lane, The Allison Inn & Spa, Newberg, OR 97132

*They say:* Creative menus accentuate the native flavors of the Willamette Valley with a strong influence on seasonality, local garden-to-table agriculture and an affinity

# Oregon Wine Pioneers

for wine pairings. Embracing thoughtful, educated service, our highly trained staff graciously offers to customize your wine pairing to complement cuisine selections.

*We say:* Upmarket dining in the heart of wine country, it's the perfect place to enjoy a sophisticated meal accompanied by thoughtfully sourced and carefully paired Oregon and international vintages.

*Don't miss:* Live jazz Friday and Saturday nights. The chance to indulge in decadent room service: get Jory's food, cocktails and wine delivered to your boudoir.

**Red Hills Market**
(971) 832-8414
155 SW 7th St, Dundee, OR 97115

*They say:* The dream of Red Hills Market began when an Oregon boy studying at the Culinary Institute of America met a Napa girl with a love of good food. Together, they traveled the world in search of place to call home. But, having seen the world the Oregon boy was drawn back to his roots and the Napa girl fell in love with the Willamette Valley. Jody and Michelle loved pairing local flavors with good food and wine and... the Oregon boy and the Napa girl built Red Hills Market.

*We say:* "A great place for wood-fired pizzas and beer," according to David Adelsheim. The short but sweet menu also features scrumptious sandwiches topped with things like Hill Farms smoked ham, spiced honey butter and gruyere cheese; and home-made olive tapenade, shaved fennel, Briar Rose chevre, and arugula. There's even PB&J for the kids.

*Don't miss:* If you're off to the Coast, or planning a hike, swing by and order a picnic basket to keep you fueled for the journey.

**Storrs Smokehouse**
(503) 538-8080
310 E 1st St, Newberg, OR 97132

*They say:* Slow cooking, quick service, casual atmosphere. This is what a smokehouse should be. Rich flavorful, fall apart tender meat smoked to perfection, locally sourced ingredients and baked from scratch biscuits. Family recipes, family name, fabulous food.

*We say:* Meat-lovers paradise that brings the great tradition of Southern barbecue to the heart of Oregon. We like that it doesn't mess around with excessive options or soft-pedal with salads. Come here to get your cave (wo)man feast on.

*Don't miss:* The Gran' Daddy plate piled with brisket, pulled pork, ribs and chicken wings. Add a side of homemade biscuits with gravy if you dare.

**The Painted Lady**
(503) 538-3850
201 S College St, Newberg, OR 97132

*They say:* At the age of 10, most Boy Scouts aren't

## Oregon Wine Pioneers

spit-roasting Cornish game hens on campouts, but such was the passion of [owner/chef] Allen Routt.... He enjoys bringing his varied influences to traditional American dishes using modern techniques to lighten them for today's palate. The Painted Lady Restaurant is where parties and celebrations take place, where familial warmth is shared. A dining destination opened out of love.

*We say:* Patrick from *Dominio IV* praises The Painted Lady's "culinary precision" and its elegant rendering of local ingredients into dishes like Oregon mushroom and spinach crepe with wild rice, lentil salad and butternut squash sauce; and smoked rainbow trout with fingerling potatoes, whole grain mustard and horseradish gelee.

*Don't miss:* Treat yourself to the tasting menu with optional wine pairing for a memorable gastronomic interpretation of the Willamette Valley. Pray the chocolate soufflé with peanut butter ice cream, peanut brittle and Pinot Noir jam is still on the dessert menu.

### Recipe
(503) 487-6853
115 N Washington St, Newberg, OR 97132

*They say:* A true neighborhood restaurant similar to those found along many villages in France, Italy and Spain. A comfortable gathering place that is known by those in the local community and sought out by travelers from both near and far.... The restaurant features reclaimed barn wood tables, refinished wood chairs, a hand-built copper top bar and warm earth tones throughout.

*We say:* Polished but friendly eatery with fine attention to detail. Simple but tasteful dishes like Pacific octopus crudo, smoked trout salad, and grilled steelhead showcase the best of Oregon's meat, fish and produce, without getting too complicated.

*Don't miss:* Keep an eye out for its pop-up dinners featuring guest chefs cooking their own unique menus, paired with wines from Recipe's cellar.

# Oregon Wine Pioneers

# McMinnville Trail Guide

# McMinnville

### Dominio IV
(503) 474-8636
888 NE 8th St, McMinnville, OR 97128

From 99W/NE Baker Street in downtown McMinnville head East on NE 8th street. Go six blocks and past the train tracks and Dominio will be on your right. Page 176.

### Ghost Hill Cellars
(503) 852-7347
12220 NE Bayliss Rd, Carlton, Oregon 97111

From 99W in Lafayette (Just North of McMinnville), head North on Bridge St. which becomes NE Abbey Road. Drive about 4 miles, then take a sharp left onto NE Oak Springs Farm Road. Page 84.

## Restaurants

### Thistle
(503) 472-9623
228 NE Evans St, McMinnville, OR 97128

*We say:* Part pioneer, part crusader, Thistle is dedicated to local and seasonal food done right. They have four main menus – one per season – giving you a perfect excuse for repeat visits.

*Don't miss:* Submit to the "chef's whim" – a multi-course tasting menu designed to be shared by the whole table. May as well take the recommended wine pairings too!

# Oregon Wine Pioneers

**La Rambla**
(503) 435-2126
238 NE 3rd St, McMinnville, OR 97128

*They say:* Named for Barcelona's famous avenue, La Rambla specializes in the cuisine of the Iberian peninsula. Our menu is full of traditional favourites as well as lesser-known delicacies awaiting discovery by intrepid diners.

*We say:* An unexpectedly authentic taste of Catalonia in downtown McMinnville with an astonishing (and award-winning) wine list that showcases a fantastic range of Willamette Valley vineyards, as well as Spanish wine proper.

*Don't miss:* Jamon serrano and jamon Iberico – god's gift to pork lovers. Inventive hot tapas like delecata squash with thyme and caraway honey, and Rioja-braised calamari.

**Gem Creole Saloon**
(503) 883-9194
236 NE 3rd St, McMinnville, OR 97128

*They say:* Creole eats. Blues. Sports. "Laisse les bons temps roulez" – Let the good times role! Relive the sounds and legendary cuisine of New Orleans – a fusion of cultures and food – a truly American creation.

*We say:* Nothing we love better than a little southern style cooking. You can't go wrong ordering things that start with "C": cornmeal catfish, crawfish étouffé, catfish two ways or the classic croque monsieur.

# McMinnville Trail Guide

*Don't miss:* Dessert. We're hard pressed to choose between the pecan pie with bourbon vanilla ice cream and the caramel bread pudding served with a shot of bourbon.

### Bistro Maison
(503) 474-1888
729 NE 3rd St, McMinnville, OR 97128

*They say:* Chef Jean-Jacques and his wife Deborah have a combined 50 years in the food and wine industry in Paris, Rome, and New York City.

*We say:* French classics paired with the best of Oregon's cellars is a compelling combination. Quirks like "build your own s'mores" for dessert just add to the charm.

*Don't miss:* Its frequent special dinners celebrating wine country highlights like harvest, crush and the International Pinot Noir Celebration.

### Nick's Italian Cafe
(503) 434-4471
521 NE 3rd St, McMinnville, OR 97128

*We say:* Almost every winemaker we met spoke fondly of Nick's. Now run by the founder's daughter Carmen Peirano, and her husband, Eric Ferguson, it remains a magnet for the industry, as well as local food and wine lovers.

*Don't miss:* Wood-fired pizzas. The home-made crusts with "a subtle flavor of fresh Italian bread" are the perfect thing for soaking up a bottle or two of Pinot.

# Oregon Wine Pioneers

# Salem

The historic meanings of the word Salem include peace, completeness, and harmony. Salem is the second most popular city name in the United States (after Franklin, and before Washington). Wineries near the capitol include *Björnson*, *Coelho*, *Illahe*, *Left Coast Cellars*, and *Whistling Dog Cellars*.

**Björnson**
(503) 877-8189
3635 Bethel Heights Rd NW, Salem, OR 97304

From Salem take the Salem-Dayton Highway/221 Northbound for about 8 miles. Take a left on Spring Valley Road. After about 1 mile take a right on Bethel Heights Road. Page 10.

From *Björnson* continue on Bethel Heights Road for 3.7 miles and take a right on Zena Road. Continue onto Lincoln-Zena Road then take a right on 99W to reach Coelho. Page 148.

Continue Northbound on Highway 221 to McMinnville. Page 218.

**Coelho**
(503) 835-9305
111 5th St, Amity, OR 97101

From Salem take 221 Northbound for about 6 miles then take a left on Zena Road. Continue onto Lincoln-Zena Road then take a right on 99W. When you enter Amity *Coelho* will be on your left on 5th. Page 148.

# Oregon Wine Pioneers

**Illahe Vineyards**
(503) 831-1248
3275 Ballard Rd, Dallas, OR 97338

From Salem take Highway 22 West to Highway 99W South toward Monmouth. After 2.7 miles take a right onto Clow Corner Road, then take a left onto Ballard Road after 2 miles. After 1.2 miles stay right on Ballard Road, and *Illahe* will be on your right. Page 136.

**Left Coast Cellars**
(503) 831-4916
4225 N Pacific Hwy W, Rickreall, OR 97371

Take Highway 22 West from Salem. After 9 miles take the 99W to Monmouth/McMinnville and turn left onto 99W headed North toward McMinnville. At four miles *Left Coast Cellars* will be on your left. Page 162.

**Whistling Dog Cellars**
(503) 329-5114
1915 NW Oak Grove Road, Salem, OR 97304

Take Highway 22 West from Salem for about 6 miles, then take a right on Oak Grove Road. Follow Oak Grove Road about 2 miles and *Whistling Dog Cellars* will be on your left. Page 98.

## Restaurants

**Luc**
(541) 753-4171
134 Southwest 4th St, Corvallis, OR

*They say:* Brian Parks and Aaron Evans do the food.

Ian Johnson runs errands, signs checks, and buys wine. we like: Champagne, Italy in general, French movies*, Sitting around, Vulgarity, Cetara, Long lunches while on vacation, Scallops Le Doge, Bursting into tears*, Mauro's wine bar in Venice, Small cars, Eating outdoors in summer, (*really only Ian likes these)

*We say:* Sense of humor + great food and wine = what's not to love? The menu offers an array of modern cooking ranging from roasted bone marrow, herb and caper salad to grilled tofu with toasted farro risotto (for those at the other end of the meat-eating spectrum).

*Don't miss:* Working your way through their wide-ranging wine list. The dinner and movie nights.

**Joel Palmer House**
(503) 864-2995
600 Ferry St, Dayton, OR 97114

*They say:* My great-grandfather, Joseph Czarnecki, opened Joe's Tavern in 1916 in Reading, PA. His son, Joseph Jr., transformed the original tavern into Joe's Restaurant, changing the focus to fine dining and wine with wild mushrooms. My parents' dream to combine fine cuisine, great mushroom hunting, and world-class wine was fully realized in 1996 when they purchased The Joel Palmer House.

*We say:* A family business going strong after four generations is a rare and beautiful thing. But the real attraction here is the food, conjured by chef/owner Chris Czarnecki from local ingredients with inspiration from the cuisines of Mexico, China, Thailand, Poland, and India.

*Don't miss:* The Mushroom Madness tasting menu – wild mushroom soup, three mushroom tart, plus non-fungal indulgences like foie gras and sturgeon.

**Blue Goat**
(503) 835-5170
506 S Trade St, Amity, OR 97101

*They say:* Savor the romance of wood-fired cooking straight from our giant hand-sculpted earthen oven. Serving the best local wine and beer in a relaxed, family-friendly environment. And featuring locally grown fresh produce, eggs, meats, and cheeses from small, sustainable farms in Oregon's Willamette Valley.

*We say:* The favorite Friday night hangout of Mark and Pattie Björnson, this cozy restaurant epitomizes easy dining. It religiously sources from local farms and producers making it a great one-stop venue for tasting Oregon's best food, wine and beer.

*Don't miss:* Wood-fired fish tacos are a spectacular fusion dish. And we love the chutzpah of the cocoa-nib crusted steak topped with singed sugared cranberries.

**Crooked House Bistro**
(503) 835-5170
506 S Trade St, Amity, OR 97101

*They say:* I believe that the experience of a good meal, paired with a good wine and enjoyable conversation, is one of life's greatest pleasures. It is my pleasure to provide the food and wine to the equation... each week we will be promoting a different Oregon winery with recommended dishes to pair with, and complement the

# Salem Trail Guide

featured wine.

*We say:* The best restaurant in Salem, according to Brad from *Illahe*. "You should go. It's this tiny purple house with maybe six tables. But chef Bernard Malherbe makes the best food" – much of it sourced from local sustainable, organic, or biodynamic farms.

*Don't miss:* Daily menus showcasing seasonal ingredients. Expect main dishes based on local beef, pork, duck and seafood; vegetarian options and cheese boards.

**Wild Pear**
(503) 378-7515
372 State St, Salem, OR 97301

*They say:* Whether it's a sit-down dinner for ten, or a cocktail reception for two thousand, our goal is to create an enjoyable and memorable experience. From amazing appetizers to decadent desserts, everything we prepare reflects our passion for Northwest cuisine. Our fun and artful restaurant in historic downtown Salem is surrounded by cool shops, galleries and fun places to explore.

*We say:* The restaurant had to be shut down and refurbished after a catastrophic water leak that damaged its historic premises, but co-owners Cecilia Ritter James and Jessica Ritter soldiered on. Now the restaurant is back you can tuck into its fresh, locally-sourced food there or to go.

## Oregon Wine Pioneers

# Southern Oregon

Experience and savor Oregon's diversity for yourself with a trip south to the Umpqua Valley, home of Abacela.

**Abacela Winery**
(541) 679-6642
12500 Lookingglass Rd, Roseburg, OR 97471

From Grants Pass take I5 Northbound to Exit 112 onto Old Highway 99 South/Dillard Highway. Follow 99 for 6.6 miles, then take a left onto Brockway Road. After 2 miles take a left onto Lookingglass Road. *Abacela* will be on your right. Page 110.

From Roseburg take I5 Southbound to Exit 119 for Highways 99 and 42. Continue on 42/99 for 2.7 miles and take a right onto NW Lookingglass Road. After about 2 miles *Abacela* will be on your right, just past Brockway Elementary School. Page 110.

## Restaurants

**Salud Restaurant & Brewery**
(541) 673-1574
537 SE Jackson St, Roseburg, OR 97470

*They say:* Created from a passion for unique Latin-inspired foods and an obsession with good craft beer. We want our restaurant to be the first place you think of for hand-crafted cocktails, shareable appetizers, tapas, and Oregon craft beers. We also showcase palate pleasing

# Southern Oregon Trail Guide

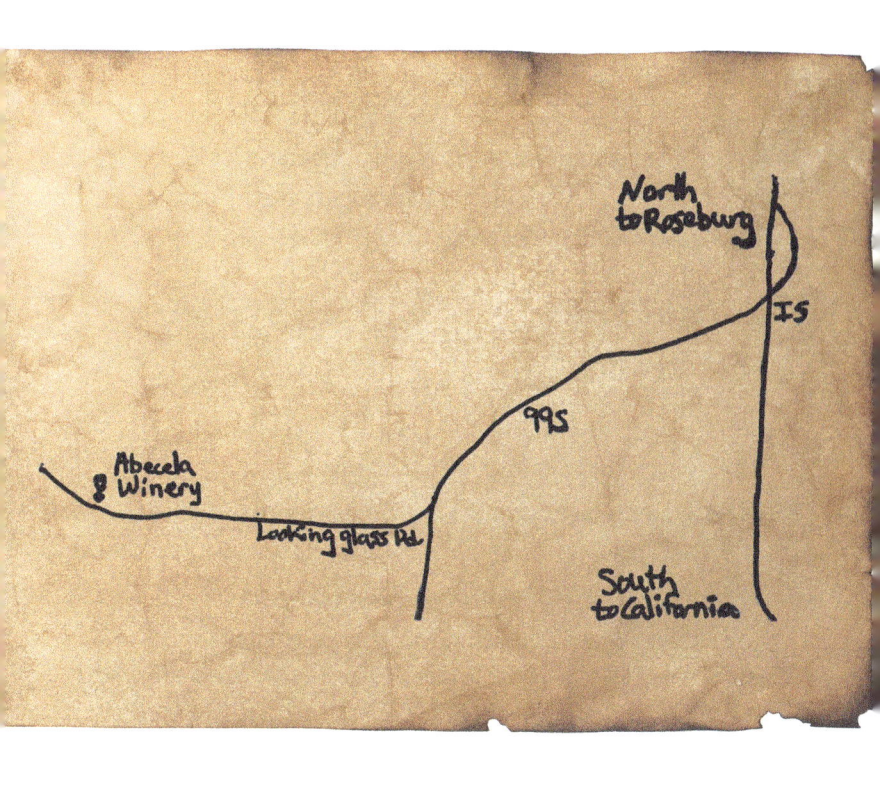

# Oregon Wine Pioneers

wines from around the Umpqua Valley. Know that we will serve you with a warm smile and energized spirit. Our atmosphere was created for laughter and relaxation.

*We say:* Easy-going but pays serious attention to food and drink. Warm up with a cocktail from their impressive drinks menu then order a bottle of local wine to accompany your Peruvian aji amarillo chicken or tacos made with Coca-Cola marinated pork.

*Don't Miss:* "Liquid dessert" – coffee laced with sweet pecan whiskey and topped with whipped cream is just the right amount of decadent to finish your meal.

**Blackbird Bistro**
(541) 672-8589
1969 SE Stephens St, Roseburg, OR 97470

*They say:* Small but elegant fine dining restaurant that emphasises local food and drink, including wine list selections from *Abacela* and *Season Cellars*. In fact, it won two medals at *Greatest of the Grape* 2015 for its food and wine pairings. Seasonal menus change every few weeks. They feature a range of high-end treats like confit duck with orange butter sauce and crème brulee alongside upscale versions of comfort food like burgers and brown sugar cheesecake.

*We say:* If you like a little rock with your dinner roll drop by for one of Blackbird's regular live music nights. It also showcases the work of local artists, giving a unique flair to its Art Deco interior.

# Southern Oregon Trail Guide

*Don't Miss:* Carnivores, get your teeth around the curried pork and bacon skewers. For a greener plate, try the roasted cauliflower salad.

**Brix**

(541) 440-4901

527 SE Jackson St, Roseburg, OR 97470

*They say:* The Brix family-owned properties are a trifecta of charming historic brick buildings that, blended together, provide a variety of upscale casual dining experiences in downtown Roseburg. Drop by for a hearty breakfast or lunch, or gather with friends for a leisurely dinner. Menus offer a variety of homemade items including comforting classics and seasonal dishes.

*We say:* A Brix breakfast is ideal fuel for a day of traveling in wine country, and it's served till 3PM. Choose from omelets, pancakes, French Toast or oatmeal – you won't need to eat again till dinner.

*Don't Miss:* Wine About It Wedesdays at Brix Chill, showcasing fine southern Oregon wines and live music.

Love and gratitude to...

Ersun for the idea and impetus behind Vine Lives, and making it happen; Carolina for support and good cheer. Congratulations to you both.

Tesan for research road-trips, a lifetime supply of magazines and so much more; Sean for winery hopping and gassing up the 4Runner; to both of you for putting me up (and putting up with me) over many years.

Ox & Rayann for sharing the joy of wine and letting me stay in the spare room.

Richard & Suzy for friendship, encouragement and generous practical assistance.

Alex @ Sa Vida Sana and Juan Carlos @ Girasol, for coffee, company and working wifi.

Simon @ Agrotourismo Morna for a beautiful home, and Robert for making it even lovelier.

*C*

---

Thanks to my lovely wife for her invaluable assistance through far too many long weekends of tedious editing sessions; thank you doubly for managing the social media campaign for the book; and thanks for reminding me that self-publishing, like the lottery, should not be engaged in for investment purposes.

Thank you Cila for doing such amazing work. It has been great. Here's hoping for another round.

Thank you Tesan for all of the advice and editing help and for the wonderful maps.

*E*